Hiking in the backcountry entails unavoidable risk that every hiker assumes and must be aware of and respect. The fact that a trail is described in this book is not a representation that it will be safe for you. Trails vary greatly in difficulty and in the degree of conditioning and agility one needs to enjoy them safely. On some hikes routes may have changed or conditions may have deteriorated since the descriptions were written. Also trail conditions can change even from day to day, owing to weather and other factors. A trail that is safe on a dry day or for a highly conditioned, agile, properly equipped hiker may be completely unsafe for someone else or unsafe under adverse weather conditions.

You can minimize your risks on the trail by being knowledgeable, prepared and alert. There is not space in this book for a general treatise on safety in the mountains, but there are a number of good books and public courses on the subject and you should take advantage of them to increase your knowledge. Just as important, you should always be aware of your own limitations and of conditions existing when and where you are hiking. If conditions are dangerous, or if you are not prepared to deal with them safely, choose a different hike! It's better to have wasted a drive than to be the subject of a mountain rescue.

These warnings are not intended to scare you off the trails. Millions of people have safe and enjoyable hikes every year. However, one element of the beauty, freedom and excitement of the wilderness is the presence of risks that do not confront us at home. When you hike you assume those risks. They can be met safely, but only if you exercise your own independent judgment and common sense.

D1495354

Painted Lady over Rae Lakes

guide to the

John Muir Trail

Thomas Winnett

 WILDERNESS PRESS • BERKELEY

FIRST EDITION February 1978
Second printing July 1979
Third printing August 1981
SECOND EDITION March 1984
Second printing June 1985
Third printing August 1986
Fourth printing April 1988
Fifth printing August 1989
Sixth printing February 1991
Seventh printing July 1992

Photos by the author except as noted
Design by the author

Library of Congress Card Catalog Number 83-51477
International Standard Book Number 0-89997-040-0
Printed in the United States of America
Published by Wilderness Press
              2440 Bancroft Way
              Berkeley CA 94704
              (510) 843-8080

Write for free catalog

Acknowledgements

If John Muir were alive, he would be at the head of the list of acknowledgements. Dead, he is still there. Muir's contagious love of the mountains afflicted all the early Sierra Club pioneers who conceived of a route from Mt. Whitney to Yosemite and inspired the building of the trail.

Among the living, my greatest debt is to Jeffrey P. Schaffer, who encouraged me to write the book, produced most of the maps and overlays, and himself mapped the trail from Rush Creek to Happy Isles. Noelle Liebrenz carefully drafted the rest of the map overlays. Ben Schifrin read the manuscript, contributing much from his fund of personal knowledge of the trail and of long-distance trekking. Jim Jenkins provided accurate mapping of the trail east of Crabtree Meadows. Jason Winnett accompanied me on the several trips needed to record a verbal description and photographs of the trail. June Menda turned my sketchy notes into exact and elegant profiles. Finally, Penelope Hargrove creatively put all the elements of finished type and art in their proper places ready for printing.

—Thomas Winnett
Berkeley, California
November 1977

"The idea of a crest-parallel trail came to me one day while herding my uncle's cattle in an immense unfenced alfalfa field near Fresno. It was 1884 and I was 14."

—Theodore S. Solomons,
"father" of the John Muir Trail

Contents

Introduction   1
The Mount Whitney Trail   9
The John Muir Trail   14
The Muir Trail Southbound   73
Trail Profiles   87
Index   101

Fin Dome over Dollar Lake

Introduction

The John Muir Trail passes through what many backpackers agree is the finest mountain scenery in the United States. Some hikers may give first prize to some other place, but none will deny the great attractiveness of the High Sierra.

This is a land of 13,000-foot and 14,000-foot peaks, of soaring granite cliffs, of lakes literally by the thousands, of canyons 5000 feet deep. It is a land where man's trails touch only a tiny portion of the total area, so that by leaving the trail you can find utter solitude. It is a land uncrossed by road for 160 airline miles from Walker Pass to Tuolumne Meadows. And perhaps best of all, it is a land blessed with the mildest, sunniest climate of any major mountain range in the world. Though rain does fall in the summer—and much snow in the winter—the rain seldom lasts more than an hour or two, and the sun is out and shining most of the hours that it is above the horizon.

Given these attractions, you might expect that quite a few people would want to enjoy them. And it is true that some hikers joke about traffic signs being needed on the John Muir Trail. But the land is so vast that if you do want to camp by yourself, you can. While following the trail in the summer, you can't avoid passing quite a few people, but you can stop to talk or not, as you choose.

This book is your guide to this wonderful mountain world. It describes the John Muir Trail from the top of Mt. Whitney to Happy Isles in Yosemite Valley, as well as the trail by which you can reach the

Muir Trail's start on Mt. Whitney. The description
and the maps are based on field work covering the
entire trail. The maps are revised U.S. Geological Sur-
vey topographic maps, corrected by Wilderness Press
to show the situation as it exists. These maps incor-
porate more than 600 changes over the existing
U.S.G.S. maps, making them the most accurate maps
of the Muir Trail available anywhere.

Planning Your Hike

The Muir Trail is not a place to hike on impulse. Its
length, its remoteness, and its great changes in alti-
tude mean that you must plan your hike if you are
going to enjoy it, or even to complete it. Before you
can even do the planning, you need considerable ex-
perience backpacking in order to find out how your
appetite behaves on long hikes, how much your body
can take without rebelling, and—particularly—how
your emotions react in various backpacking situations.
For example, you will have your own typical reac-
tions to solitude (if you go alone), enforced together-
ness (if you don't go alone), cold, hunger and injury.

Once you know these things, you're ready to plan
your Muir Trail hike. To estimate how long it will
take you, divide your typical day's mileage into 210
to get the number of days you will be hiking. Add the
number of layover days you think you would like to
take, and you have the total elapsed days. Then, using
the mileage chart at the end of this chapter, you can
figure just about where you will be every night if you
stick to your schedule.

Supplies

Almost no one hikes the whole Muir Trail without
resupplying. You don't need to, since there are two
places with stores almost exactly en route—Reds
Meadow and Tuolumne Meadows. However, these
stores don't carry much food that's really suitable for

backpacking. At Tuolumne Meadows, that doesn't matter much, because you can eat a couple of satisfying meals on store-bought food or at the coffee shop or in the lodge, and then, in about two days, be in Yosemite Valley at the end of your trek. So the problem is the roughly 200 miles from Whitney Portal to Tuolumne Meadows. If you hike very strenuously, you might average 17+ miles a day. Then you could finish in 12 days, if you hiked every day. If you need two pounds of food per day, and your non-food pack weighs 30 pounds, you will start with 54 pounds, a fairly manageable pack.

However, most people will average more like 12 miles a day, will layover for a couple of days, and will therefore take perhaps 19 or 20 days. Based on the same assumptions, a pack for that trip would at the start weigh almost 70 pounds, which for at least some of us is quite a load to carry up the 5300 vertical feet from Whitney Portal to Trail Crest.

The answer to this problem is one of three: cache some food in the wilderness beforehand; mail some food to yourself at a post office near the route, or go out to a town to resupply. The best town to resupply is in Bishop. From a junction 79 miles from Whitney Portal, you can hike northeast 12 miles to South Lake, which has nothing but a parking lot, and hitchhike 22 miles to Bishop. From a junction 24 miles farther, you can hike northeast 18 miles to North Lake, similarly undeveloped, and hitchhike 20 miles to Bishop. If you choose to mail, the nearest mail place is Vermilion Valley Resort, at the foot of Lake Thomas Edison. Leave the Muir Trail beside the Mono Creek bridge and walk 6 miles west to the resort, which has a small store plus meals, showers and a package-holding service. They also operate a boat-taxi the length of Lake Edison, which can save you much walking. Write ahead to confirm the services and the conditions. (Enclose a SASE.)

> Vermilion Valley Resort
> C/o Rancheria Garage
> Huntington Lake Road
> Lakeshore, CA 93634

In terms of elapsed time from the Muir Trail to a post office, the nearest one is Mammoth Lakes (93546), reached by an hour's hitchhike (if you're lucky) from Reds Meadow, or an hour's bus ride from there plus time waiting for the bus—if it is in service. The town of Mammoth Lakes has plenty of supplies.

When mailing your package to any of these places, address it to:

> Yourself
> General Delivery
> P.O., state ZIP
> HOLD UNTIL (date)

Before you leave home, write the post office you will be sending mail to, to make sure they will hold your mail for your arrival. They are legally required to hold it *only* 10 days. Also find out what hours they are open. Finally, don't mail perishables.

Wilderness Permits

If you are walking north, you can get a permit for the whole John Muir Trail from the Forest Service. Write Mt. Whitney District Ranger, P.O. Box 8, Lone Pine, CA 93545. If you are walking south, you can get a permit for the whole trail from Yosemite. Write between Feb. 1 and May 31 to Backcountry Office, Box 577, Yosemite National Park, CA 95389. After May 31, obtain it in person in Yosemite Valley at the Park headquarters.

Animal Problems

Experienced backpackers know not to leave food around where rodents can get at it, and they know that in bear country they must take special precautions. (You can expect to encounter bears on almost any part of the Muir Trail). Rodents will chew their way into packs if the packs are tightly laced but unattended. Bears will perform near-miracles to get your goodies. As more and more people have taken up backpacking, there has been more and more unnatural food for bears—the food brought in by backpackers. Since this food is attractive to bears, and all too often easily available, the animals have developed a habit of seeking it and eating it. They patrol popular campsites nightly. As the bears have become more knowledgeable and persistent, backpackers have escalated their food-protecting methods. From merely putting it in one's pack by one's bed at night, and chasing away any bear that came, backcountry travelers switched to hanging the food over a branch of a tree. But bears can climb trees, and they can gnaw or scratch through the nylon line that you tie around a tree trunk. When they sever the line, the food hanging from the other end of the line of course falls to the ground. This happens all too often in Yosemite Park.

To avoid food loss due to line severance, you can learn the *counterbalance* method of "bearbagging." First, tie a small stone to the end of a 30-foot length of nylon line (1/8" or so in diameter) as a weight to hurl up and over a likely branch. The branch should be at least 16 feet up, and long enough that the line can rest securely at a point at least six feet from the tree trunk. When you have the line over the branch, tie a bag with half your food to one end of the line. Now pull it up to the branch. Then tie a second food bag to the other end of the line, as high as you can reach. Now, using a stick, make the two bags equally high, at least 10 feet off the ground. Next morning push up either bag until the other descends to where you can reach it.

In recent years rangers have placed "bear boxes" at a number of popular campsites along the Muir Trail. These can replace hanging your food.

REMEMBER: If a bear does get your food, he will then consider it his, and he will fight any attempts you make to retrieve it. Don't try! Remember also never to leave your food unprotected even for a short while during the daytime.

Giardia

This protozoan can cause acute gastrointestinal distress. The illness is treatable, but prevention is best. I recommend that you treat all water to be sure. Filtration, boiling and additives should all work if conscientiously done.

Summer Rangers

To help you cope with difficulties and to see that hikers heed the rules for preserving the wilderness, a number of summer rangers are stationed along the trail in Sequoia and Kings Canyon National Parks, and sometimes at Rush Creek Forks, from about July 4 to Labor Day. The trail description below tells where they are. Two points deserve special mention. First, if you go to a summer ranger station to report a friend in trouble and find the ranger out, please realize he might be gone for several days, so leave a note for him and walk out for help yourself. Second, remember that the ranger has to buy his own food and camping gear, so he, not the government, is the loser if it is taken.

No-Fire Zones

Fires are not permitted above 9600 feet in Yosemite, 10,000 feet in Kings Canyon or 11,200 feet in Sequoia National Park.

Cumulative Mileage Table

	South to North		North to South
Mt. Whitney Summit	0.0		209.8
		2.0	
Mt. Whitney Trail	2.0		207.8
		6.0	
Crabtree Ranger Station	8.0		201.8
		1.3	
Pacific Crest Trail	9.3		200.5
		3.3	
Wallace Creek	12.6		197.2
		5.3	
Lake South America Trail	17.9		191.9
		4.3	
Forester Pass	22.2		187.6
		8.0	
Bubbs Creek Trail	30.2		179.6
		2.2	
Kearsarge Pass Trail	32.4		177.4
		2.3	
Glen Pass	34.7		175.1
		8.3	
Woods Creek	43.0		166.8
		7.1	
Pinchot Pass	50.1		159.7
		4.3	
South Fork Kings River	54.4		155.4
		5.2	
Mather Pass	59.6		150.2
		10.2	
Middle Fork Kings River	69.8		140.0
		3.3	
Bishop Pass Trail	73.1		136.7
		7.0	
Muir Pass	80.1		129.7
		4.6	
Evolution Lake Inlet	84.7		125.1
		7.1	
Evolution Creek in Evolution Meadow	91.8		118.0
		5.1	
Piute Pass Trail	96.9		112.9
		1.8	
Florence Lake Trail	98.7		111.1
		7.6	
Selden Pass	106.3		103.5
		14.7	
Mono Creek	121.0		88.8
		7.0	
Silver Pass	128.0		81.8
		4.8	
Tully Hole	132.8		77.0
		6.3	
Duck Lake outlet	139.1		70.7
		11.6	
Reds Meadow	150.7		59.1
		9.6	
Shadow Lake	160.3		49.5
		5.5	
Thousand Island Lake outlet	165.8		44.0
		3.3	
Rush Creek Forks	169.1		40.7
		3.8	
Donohue Pass	172.9		36.9
		4.0	
Lyell Base Camp	176.9		32.9
		9.6	
Highway 120 in Tuolumne Meadows	186.5		23.3
		1.2	
Recrossing of the highway	187.7		22.1
		3.8	
Lateral to lower Cathedral Lake	191.5		18.3
		4.6	
Sunrise High Sierra Camp	196.1		13.7
		9.3	
Little Yosemite Valley	205.4		4.4
		4.4	
Happy Isles	209.8		0.0

The scale of maps in this book is 1:67,760, or 1'' equals 1.1 miles approx.

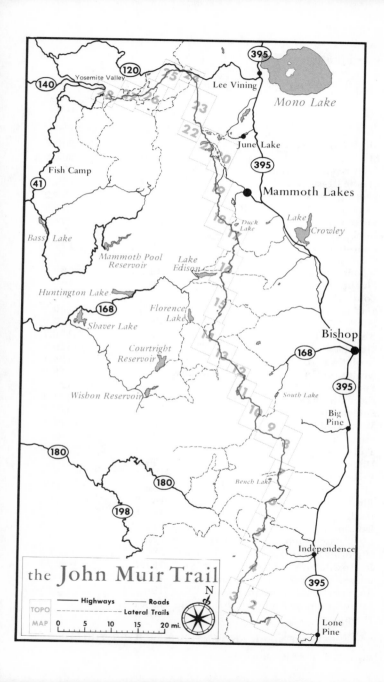

the **John Muir Trail**

The Mt. Whitney Trail

In the trail descriptions that follow, you will often find a pair of numbers in parentheses. The first number is the elevation at that point; the second number is the mileage since the last such point.

The numbers on each page of trail description refer to the map(s) that cover the area being described on that page.

Literally, the John Muir Trail connects the top of Mt. Whitney with Yosemite Valley. But of course you can't drive to the top of Mt. Whitney. Therefore this description of the Muir Trail begins at Whitney Portal, a road end 13 miles west of Lone Pine, California, where there is adequate parking, a campground, and a small store and cafe.

1

From just east of a small store (8361') the route follows the old stock trail from the defunct pack station as it steadily climbs through a moderate forest cover of Jeffrey pine and red fir. After ½ mile the trail crosses North Fork Lone Pine Creek and shortly enters the John Muir Wilderness, beyond the junction with the abandoned foottrail section. Soon the forest cover thins, and the slope is covered with a chaparral that includes mountain mahogany, Sierra chinquapin and sagebrush. This steep slope can get very hot in midmorning, and the trip is best begun as early as possible. Breather stops on this trail section provide a "Veed" view down the canyon framing the Alabama Hills—a filming location for many western movies.

The trail then turns south and levels off somewhat through several willow-covered pockets having a moderate forest cover of lodgepole and foxtail pines. It passes fields of corn lilies, delphinium, tall lupine and swamp whiteheads as it approaches a ford of Lone Pine Creek—your first water in late season. Shortly beyond this log ford is a junction (10,080 − 2.4) with a spur trail that leads east to Lone Pine Lake, which you can glimpse through the trees. Soon the trail turns west up a barren wash and reaches the soggy lower end of Outpost Camp (called "Bighorn Park" on the topo map), a willow-covered meadow that was once a little lake.

At the upper end of the meadow our trail veers away from the waterfall that tumbles down into Outpost Camp from the southwest, crosses Lone Pine Creek on a log again, and makes a short series of switchbacks beside the cascading creek, past blossoming creambush, Indian paintbrush, Sierra chinquapin, Newberry's penstemon, currant, pennyroyal, fireweed and senecio. Just after the trail crosses a footbridge, it arrives at Mirror Lake (10,650 − 1.6), cradled in its cirque beneath the south face of Thor Peak. This cold lake has fair fishing for rainbow and brook trout, but camping is no longer allowed here.

Leaving Mirror Lake, the trail ascends the south wall of the cirque via switchbacks that rise to timberline. At the top of the ascent, a last foxtail pine and a broken, weathered, convoluted whitebark snag are seen, along with a few last willows. Some very spartan, small campsites can be found a short distance south of the trail. Soon Mt. Whitney comes into view over Pinnacle Ridge. From here the rocky trail ascends moderately alongside the gigantic boulders on the north side of South Fork Lone Pine Creek. In the cracks in the boulders, the hiker will find ivesia, cinquefoil, creambush, currant, and much gooseberry, and looking across the canyon he will see the cascading outlet of large Consultation Lake. Beside a rock

Thor Peak over Mirror Lake

bridge that crosses the stream are specimens of the moisture-loving shooting star.

After ascending over some poured concrete steps, the hiker arrives at the last campsites before the west side of the Sierra crest, at Trail Camp (12,000 − 2.0). Here beneath Wotan's Throne is also the last reliable water in late season. There are numerous level campsites but no wood. Then, as the trail begins exactly 100 switchbacks to the pass (called Trail Crest), Mt. Whitney is occluded by a sharp spire, and Mt. Russell, farther north and also over 14,000 feet, comes into view The rocky, barren talus slope we are panting up is not *entirely* barren, for in season one may see a dozen species of flowering plants, climaxed by the multiflowered, blue "sky pilot." The building of this trail section required much blasting with dynamite, and the natural fracture planes of the granite are evident in the blasted slabs. Finally the grueling 1600-foot ascent from Trail Camp ends at Trail Crest (13,600 − 2.2), and the hiker suddenly has vistas of a great part of Sequoia National Park to the west, including the entire Great Western Divide. Close underneath in the west are the two long Hitchcock Lakes. To the east, far below, are Consultation Lake and several smaller, unnamed lakes lying close under the Whitney Crest. These lakes may not be free of ice the whole summer.

From the pass, our trail descends on a gentle gradient along a very steep mountainside to meet the John Muir Trail (13,560 − 0.2). Turning right on it, we begin the last two slogging miles to the summit of Mt. Whitney. As we wind among the large blocks of talus, we often have views, through notch-windows, of Owens Valley, 10,000 feet below us in the east. Closer below are the heads of barren glacial cirques, most of them containing brilliant turquoise lakes. Finally, we see ahead on an almost level plateau a

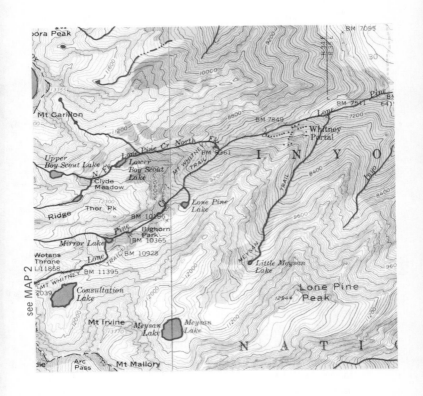

small cabin near the summit, and with a well-earned
feeling of accomplishment we take the last few steps **2**
to the highest point in the "lower 48" states (14,495
− 2.0).

The John Muir Trail

The John Muir Trail begins—or ends, as you choose —at the top of Mt. Whitney. If you hike the Muir Trail southbound, you will end up on this peak. To get down to civilization near Lone Pine, follow the description of Chapter 2 in reverse. If you hike the Muir Trail northbound to Yosemite Valley, follow the description of Chapter 3.

From the summit of Mt. Whitney (14,495 − 0.0) your trail descends south for two miles, passing numerous viewpoints where the trail comes close to the top of a notch that is the head of a very steep eastside chute incised into the Sierra crest. You also pass within 400 feet of the summit of a 14,000-foot peak named for John Muir, Mt. Muir, about 1½ miles south of Whitney. Then you reach the junction with the Mt. Whitney Trail (13,560 − 2.0) and turn right. From this junction the trail descends 1500 vertical feet via a long set of rocky switchbacks. The population pressure on this trail segment is evidenced by the frequent bedsites constructed in the mountain wall, especially near switchback hairpins. Beside the trail, large yellow flowers called hulsea, or "Alpine gold," have anchored themselves in the most unlikely-looking places.

Breathing thicker air, we reach the bottom of the switchbacks and head northwest across tundra, passing an unnamed lakelet on a gentle-to-moderate descent. Then your trail swings close to the north shore of Guitar Lake (11,500 − 3.0) and crosses the inlet creek on boulders. In early season, you may see large

golden trout swimming upstream from the lake to
spawn, their bodies too thick to be covered entirely
by the water of this small stream. Across the lake we
have excellent views of the avalanche-scarred north
face of Mt. Hitchcock. The avalanche chutes end part-
way down the face; their lower portions were
smoothed off by the passage of the most recent glacier, and have not had time to redevelop since then.
Soon your trail reaches timberline, and then descends
through a little canyon to small, reflective Timberline Lake (11,070 − 1.1) (no camping). The bulk of
Mt. Whitney mirrored in the lake is quite photogenic.

2

see MAP 4

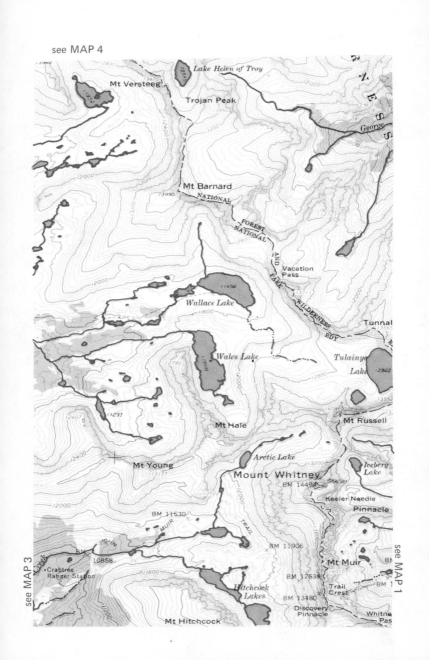

see MAP 3

see MAP 1

From this lake the trail rises northwest over a small ridge and then descends to boulder-hop a small stream. In about ¼ mile you reach a meadow that has some very pleasant campsites. Continuing down the creek's canyon, you soon pass Crabtree Ranger Station (10,640 — 1.9), where a ranger is on duty in the summer—when he is not out on patrol. Just beyond this outpost, a trail veers left to Crabtree Meadows and your trail passes near some adequate campsites. From the ford, the trail quickly rises diagonally up a sandy slope forested by large foxtail pines, and then follows the contour line west to a junction with the Pacific Crest Trail (10,880 — 1.3). Here we turn right and soon descend to a mapped stream that stops flowing in early summer. Then, leaving the foxtail forest—ghostly on an overcast day—you skirt what the map calls Sandy Meadow and ascend to a high saddle (10,964 — 1.7). Beyond it the trail winds among the huge boulders of a glacial moraine on the west shoulder of Mt. Young and brings you to excellent viewpoints for scanning the main peaks of the Kings-Kern Divide and of the Sierra crest from Mt. Barnard (13,990 feet) north to Junction Peak (13,888 feet). Soon you descend moderately, making several easy fords, and then switchback down to Wallace Creek and a junction (10,390 — 1.6) where the High Sierra Trail goes west toward a roadend near Giant Forest and a lateral trail goes east to Wallace Lake. The Wallace Creek ford, just north of the popular campsites, is difficult in early season.

Now your sandy trail climbs up to a forested flat, crosses it, and reaches the good campsite at the ford of Wright Creek (10,790 — 1.1), also difficult in early season. You then trace a bouldery path across the ground moraines left by the Wright Creek glacier and

2

3

rise in several stages to Bighorn Plateau. Views from here are indeed panoramic. An unnamed, grass-fringed lake atop the gravelly, lupine-streaked plateau makes for great morning photographs westward over it. Now the John Muir Trail descends the talus-clad west slope of Tawny Point past many extraordinarily dramatic foxtail pines. At an unnamed lake beside the trail there are fair campsites and warmish swimming, but hardly any wood. At the foot of this rocky slope a trail goes southwest one half mile to a summer ranger station and then on to the Kern River, and 200 yards past the junction you come to the unsigned Shepherd Pass Trail (10,930 − 3.5) going northeast. Immediately beyond is a formidable ford of Tyndall Creek. A short way down the creek is a summer ranger station, manned in some years.

3
4

From these gathering places your trail makes a short climb to the junction with the Lake South America Trail (11,160 − 0.7), passes some fair campsites, and rises above timberline. As you tackle the ascent to the highest pass on the John Muir Trail, you wind among the barren basins of high, rockbound, but fish-filled lakes to the foot of a great granite wall, then labor up numerous switchbacks, some of which

Great Western Divide from Bighorn Plateau

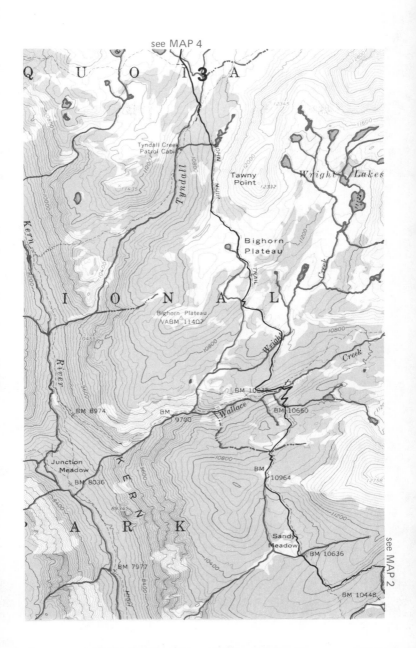

see MAP 2

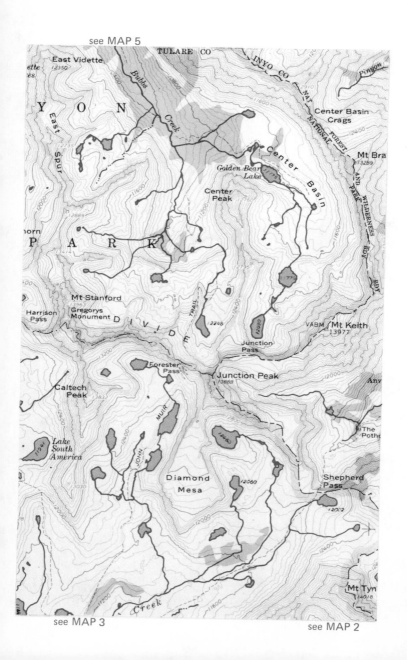

see MAP 5

TULARE CO

INYO CO

East Vidette
12350

East Spur

Bubbs Creek

Center Basin Crags

NATIONAL FOREST

Mt Bra
13289

Golden Bear Lake

Center Basin

Center Peak

AND PARK WILDERNESS BDY

12889

P A R K

BDY

horn

Mt Stanford
Gregorys Monument D

Harrison Pass

D I V I D E

TRAIL

12248

12060

Junction Pass

VABM Mt Keith
13977

Caltech Peak

Forester Pass

Junction Peak
12888

MUIR

Anv

The Poth

JOHN

Lake South America

Diamond Mesa

12060

Shepherd Pass

13002

see MAP 3

Creek

Mt Tyn
14018

see MAP 2

are literally cut into the rock wall, to Forester Pass
(13,180 − 4.3), on the border between Sequoia and
Kings Canyon National Parks. Wearing your wind gar-
ment, you will enjoy the well-earned, sweeping views
from this pass. Down the switchbacks you go, unless
they are buried under snow, and then stroll high above
the west shore of Lake 12248. The trail soon doubles
back to ford splashing Bubbs Creek just below that
lake, then fords it twice more within a mile. Soon you
reach timber, ford Center Basin creek (high in early
season), pass the Center Basin Trail (10,500 − 4.5)
and then ford more tributaries of Bubbs Creek. Many
good campsites are located near some of these fords
and along the main creek, but wood is scarce, as it is
almost everywhere along the Muir Trail.

4

Continuing down the east side of dashing Bubbs
Creek, you reach Vidette Meadow (9600 − 2.8), long
a favorite camping spot in these headwaters of South
Fork Kings River. High use has made the place less
attractive, but its intrinsic beauty has not been lost,
and the mighty Kearsarge Pinnacles to the northeast
have lost only a few inches of height at most since
Sierra Club founders like Joseph Le Conte camped

5

Forester Pass from the south

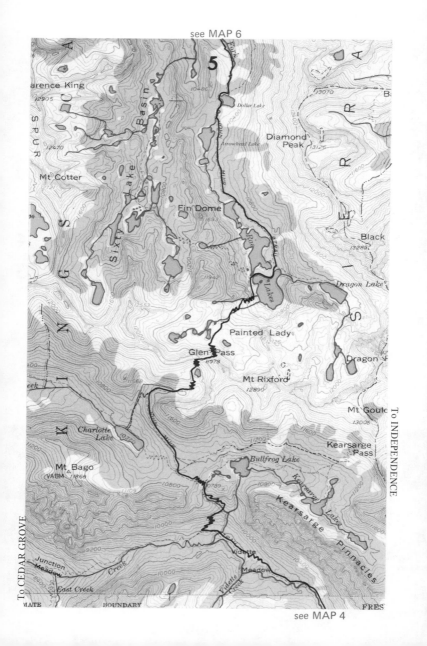

5

To CEDAR GROVE

To INDEPENDENCE

Clarence King
12905

SPUR

12470

Mt Cotter

SIXTY

Sixty Lake

Basin

KINGS

Charlotte Lake

Mt Bago
VABM

Junction
Meadow

East Creek

MATE   BOUNDARY

Dollar Lake

Arrowhead Lake

Fin Dome
10693

Rae

11942

12553

Painted Lady
12126

Glen Pass
11978

Mt Rixford
12890

Diamond
Peak
13126

13070

Black
13289

Dragon Lake

Dragon

Mt Goulc
13005

Kearsarge
Pass

Bullfrog Lake

Kearsarge Lakes

Kearsarge Pinnacles

Vidette
Meadow

Creek

FRES

here at the turn of the century. Camping is limited
to one night in one place from here to Woods Creek.
A summer ranger is in Vidette Meadow east of the
trail to assist traffic flow.

Beyond the meadow, a trail goes west to Cedar
Grove and the Muir Trail turns north (9550 − 0.7) to
fiercely attack the wall of Bubbs Creek canyon. You
pause for breath at the Bullfrog Lake junction (10,530
− 1.5) and then finish off the tough climb at a broad,
sandy saddle that contains the junction of the Charlotte Lake and Kearsarge Pass trails (10,710 − 0.7).
There are modest supplies at the Kearsarge roadend in
Onion Valley, and a summer ranger on the east shore
of Charlotte Lake. In one-fourth mile you pass a shortcut (for southbound hikers) to the Kearsarge Pass
Trail, and then you traverse high above emerald Charlotte Lake. As the route veers eastward, it passes another trail to Charlotte Lake, then climbs past a talus-
choked pothole and ascends gently to the foot of the
wall that is notched by Glen Pass. It is hard to see
where a trail could go up that precipitous blank wall,
but one does, and after very steep switchbacks you
are suddenly at Glen Pass (11,978 − 2.3). The view
north presents a barren, rocky, brown world with pre-
cious little green of tree or meadow visible. Yet you
know by now that not far down the trail ahead there
will be plenty of willows, sedges, wildflowers and,
eventually, groves of whitebark, lodgepole and foxtail pines. To be sure you get there, take special care
on your descent from Glen Pass as you switchback
down to a small lake basin, ford the lakes' outlet and
switchback down again.

When you are about 400 vertical feet above Rae
Lakes, you will see why Dragon Peak (12,995'), in
the southeast, has that name. Where the 60 Lakes
Trail turns off to the west (10,550 − 2.0) your route
turns east, crosses the isthmus between two of the

5

see MAP 7

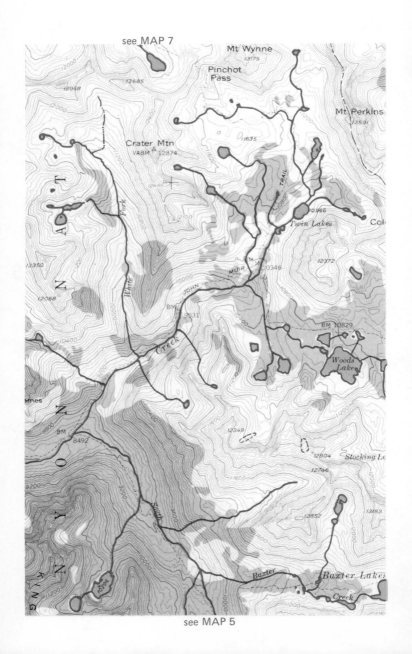

see MAP 5

Rae Lakes, passes the Dragon Lake Trail, and winds above the east short of the middle lake, passing a summer ranger station. As of this writing, wood fires are not allowed between Glen Pass and the Baxter Pass Trail. Beyond Rae Lakes your gently descending trail passes above an unnamed lake and drops to the northeast corner of aptly named Arrowhead Lake, where there is good camping. Then it fords gurgling South Fork Woods Creek on boulders and reaches scenic, heavily used Dollar Lake. The unsigned Baxter Pass Trail heads northeast from below the outlet of this lake (10,230 − 2.6).

From the Baxter Pass Trail you descend gently down open, lightly forested slopes, crossing several good-sized though unnamed streams, including the bridged creek from Lake 10296. The reward for all this descent is a chance to start climbing again at Woods Creek (8492 − 3.7), crossed on a wood bridge, where the campsites are good but much used. Immediately beyond the bridge a trail to Cedar Grove goes south down the creek. As you perspire north from

5

6

Just south of Pinchot Pass

the crossing up the valley of Woods Creek, there is no drinking-water problem, what with the main stream near at hand and many tributaries, some of good size, to jump or boulder-hop. After the junction of the Sawmill Pass Trail (10,370 − 3.4), the grade abates and the traveler reaches the alpine vale where this branch of the Kings River has its headwaters, bounded by glorious peaks on 3½ sides. With one last, long spur you finally top Pinchot Pass (12,130 − 3.7), one of those "passes" that are regretably not at the low point of the divide.

From this pass the Muir Trail swoops down into the lake-laden valley below, runs along the east shore of at-timberline Lake Marjorie, touches its outlet (11,160 − 1.7), and then passes four lakelets, fording several small streams along the way. A summer ranger station is located beyond the fourth lakelet, just south of the Bench Lake Trail junction. Bench Lake, on a true bench high above South Fork Kings River's canyon, has good campsites that are off the beaten track. Just beyond this junction we ford the outlet of Lake Marjorie and in 200 yards meet the Taboose Pass Trail (10,750 − 1.3) at the upper edge of a lodgepole forest. Another downhill segment of forested switchbacks brings you to the South Fork, which is best crossed on a log 100 yards upstream from the trail. On the far bank the South Fork Trail (10,050 − 1.3) leads downstream and you turn northeast upstream, passing another trail to Taboose Pass in one-third mile. Climbing steadily, you cross several unnamed tributaries that can slow you down at the height of the melt, and then ford the infant South Fork (10,840 − 2.2) near some good campsites. East of the trail, on the Sierra crest, looming Cardinal Mountain (13,397′) is named for red but is in fact half white and half dark, in a strange mixture of metamorphosed Paleozoic rocks. West of this peak you cross grassy flats and hop over numerous branches of

see MAP 8

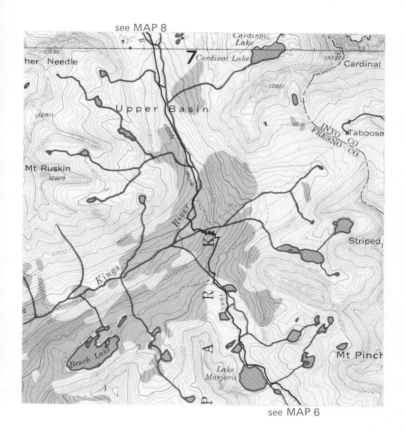

see MAP 6

the headwaters of South Fork Kings River. Every camper can have his own lake or lakelet in this high basin—though the campsites are austere.

This ascent finally steepens and zigzags up to rock-bound Mather Pass (12,100 − 3.0), named for Stephen Mather, first head of the National Park Service. The view ahead is dominated by the 14,000-foot peaks of the Palisades group, knifing sharply into the sky. Your trail now makes a knee-shocking descent to the poor campsites one-fourth mile southeast of long, blue upper Palisade Lake. The route then con-

8

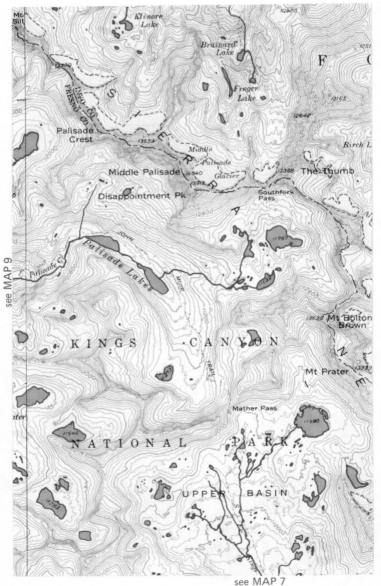

see MAP 9

see MAP 7

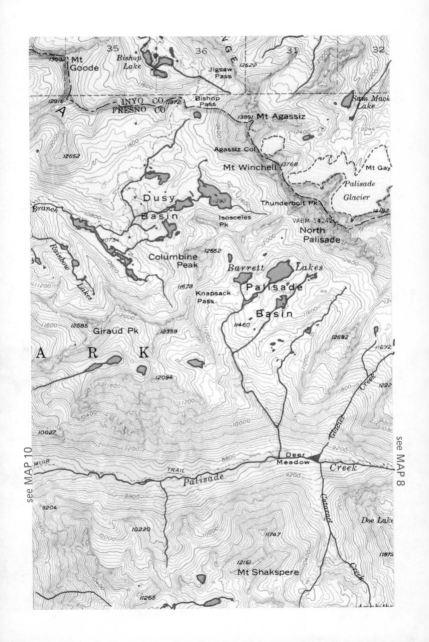

tours above the lakes until it drops to the north shore of the lower lake (10,600 − 3.5), with its poor-to-fair campsites, Knees rested, you descend again, down the

8 "Golden Staircase," built on the cliffs of the gorge of Palisade Creek. This section was the last part of the Muir Trail to be constructed, and it is easy to see why. In three-fourths mile from the bottom of the "staircase" you cross multibranched Glacier Creek and immediately arrive at Deer Meadow (8860 − 3.0), which is more lodgepole forest than meadow, but

9 pleasant enough anyway. Beyond the campsites here, the downhill grade continues, less steeply, across the stream draining Palisade Basin and several smaller streams to reach Middle Fork Kings River (8020 − 3.7), where a trail takes off down-stream for Simpson Meadow. Turning north, you ascend past a series of

10 falls and chutes along the river to Grouse Meadows, a serene expanse of grassland with good campsites in the forest along the east side. Up the canyon from

Grouse Meadows

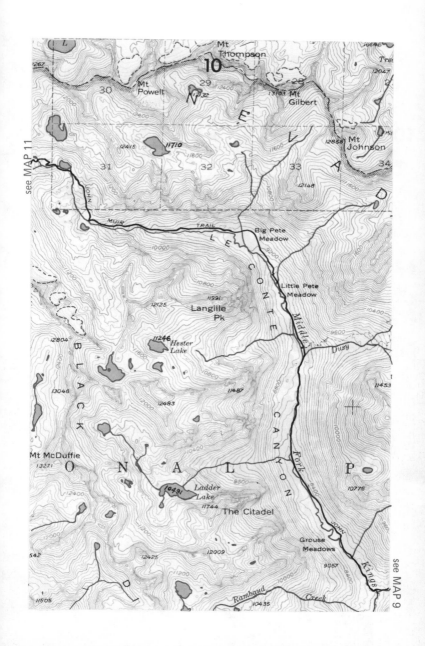

10

Mt Thompson

Mt Powell

Mt Gilbert

Mt Johnson

Mt McDuffie

Big Pete Meadow

Little Pete Meadow

Langille Pk

Hester Lake

Ladder Lake

The Citadel

Grouse Meadows

Rambaud Creek

MUIR TRAIL

JOHN

LE CONTE CANYON

BLACK

DONALD

Middle Fork

Dusy

Kings

1267
10846
12047
30
29
32
28
13103
13191
31
12415
11710
32
11600
33
12868
34
12148
12125
10000
10800
11991
12804
11246
13046
11457
12483
13271
12400
542
11505
10491
11744
12009
12425
12009
11200
10435
9000
9600
10400
11453
9500
10776
9957
10000
11400

these meadows, you can see repeated evidence of great avalanches that crashed down the immense canyon walls and wiped out stands of trees. The trail climbs gently to turbulent Dusy Branch, crossed on a steel bridge, and immediately encounters the Bishop Pass Trail (8710 − 3.3) to South Lake. Near this junction is a ranger station manned in summer.

Our route up-canyon from this junction ascends between highly polished granite walls past lavish displays of a great variety of wildflowers in season. The trail passes beside sagebrush-clothed Little Pete and Big Pete Meadows (the former is bigger) and swings

10

Dynamited trail above Big Pete Meadow

Muir Hut at Muir Pass

west to assault the Goddard Divide and search out its
breach, Muir Pass. Up and up the rocky trail winds,
passing the last tree long before you reach desolate
Helen Lake (11,595 – 5.7), named, along with Wanda
Lake to the west, for John Muir's daughters. This
east side of the pass is under snow throughout the
summer in some years.

Finally, after 5 fords of the diminishing stream,
you haul up at Muir Pass (11,955 – 1.3), where a
stone hut honoring Muir would shelter you fairly well
in a storm, though the roof leaks. The views from
here of the solitary peaks and lonely lake basins are
painted in the many hues of the mostly Jurassic-age
metamorphic rocks that make up the Goddard Divide.

From the hut your trail descends gently past Lake
McDermand and Wanda Lake, the latter having fair
though treeless campsites near its outlet. (Wood fires
are banned from Muir Pass to beyond Evolution
Lake.) You then ford Evolution Creek (11,400 –
2.2) and descend into the Sapphire Lake Basin, where

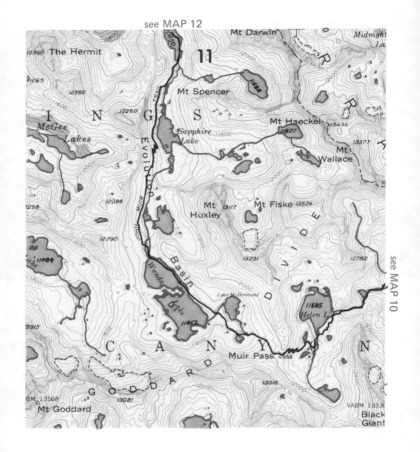

11

there are fair campsites on the north end of Sapphire Lake. The land here is nearly as scoured as when the ice left it about 100 years ago, and the aspect all around is one of newborn nakedness. To the east is a series of tremendous peaks named for Charles Darwin and other major thinkers about evolution, and the next lake and the valley below it also bear the name "Evolution."

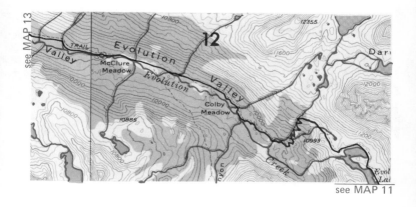

12

see MAP 11

Mt. Darwin from near Sapphire Lake

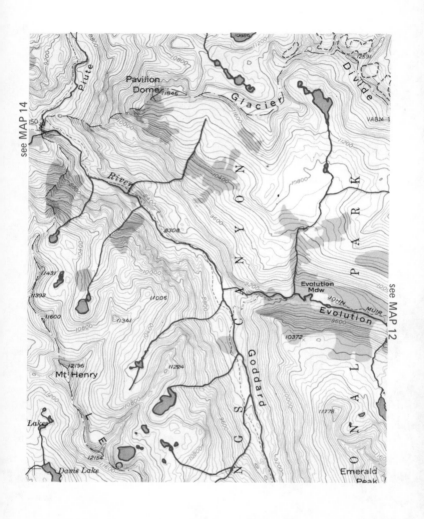

see MAP 14

see MAP 12

11

The trail fords the stream (difficult in early season and sometimes mid) at the inlet (10,850 − 2.4) of this long lake, which has some campsites in stands of stunted whitebark pines at the north end. A few hundred yards from them, at a switchback, you pass the beginning of the unsigned trail up to Darwin Canyon and over Lamarck Col, then drop sharply into Evolution Valley. The marvelous meadows in this valley are the reason for a rerouting of the trail through the forest, so the fragile grasslands can recover from overtromping by the feet of earlier backpackers and horsepackers. After crossing the multibranched **12** stream that drains Darwin Canyon, you pass Colby Meadow, with many good campsites. Farther along, at McClure Meadow (9650 − 4.9) you will find a summer ranger midway along the meadow. After further descent and several boulder fords of tributaries, you **13** skirt Evolution Meadow and come to a crossing of Evolution Creek (9240 − 2.5), which may be difficult in early season. After passing overlooks of some

The log crossing below Evolution Meadow (ephemeral)

13

beautiful falls and cascades on the creek, the trail switchbacks steeply down to the South Fork San Joaquin River's canyon floor and detours upstream to find a long bridge (8470 − 1.0). Again headed down-

Evolution Creek below Evolution Meadow

stream, you pass numerous campsites, recross the
river on another bridge, and stroll past the many
campsites at Aspen Flat. From this hospitable riverside slope, you roll on down and out of Kings Canyon
National Park at the steel-bridge crossing of Piute
Creek, where the Piute Pass Trail (8050 − 3.8) goes
north to North Lake.

13

The John Muir Trail continues down the South
Fork canyon, away from the river, to a junction with
the Florence Lake Trail (7890 − 1.8). The Florence
Lake roadend is 11 miles west down this trail; the
Muir Trail Ranch resort is 1½ miles down it. (The
latter is a possible package drop; inquire of the own-
er, Adeline Smith, by writing Box 176, Lakeshore,
CA 93634 from mid-June to October or Box 269,
Ahwahnee, CA 93601 in other months. Enclose a self-
addressed stamped envelope. Shortly before the ranch,
and about 200 yards west of signs that indicate the
John Muir Trail is 1½ miles away, both to the east and
to the north, an unsigned trail goes south ¼ mile down
to riverside campsites. From the campsites on the
south side of the river a faint trail goes 150 yards
southwest to a natural hot-spring pool—great for
soaking off the grime—and a warmish small lake—
great for rinsing off.

14

Hot pool near Blaney Meadows

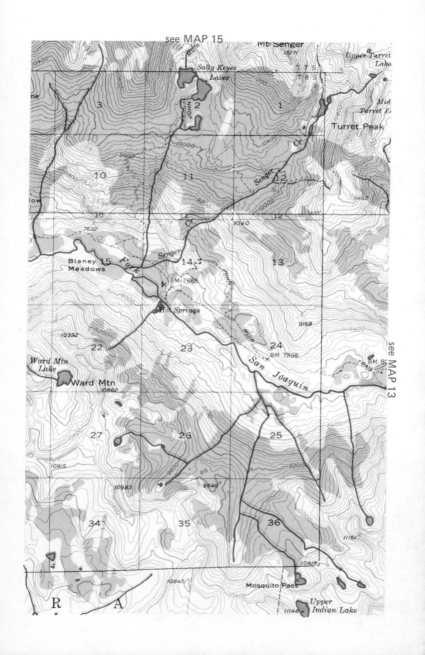

see MAP 15

see MAP 13

From the Florence Lake Trail junction, the John Muir Trail veers right to climb the canyon wall. It rises past a lateral trail down to the Florence Lake Trail (8400 − 1.7), crosses little Senger Creek (9740 − 2.2), levels off, and in a large meadow just below Sally Keyes Lakes meets another trail (10,150 − 1.6) down to the river valley below. Then your route passes the good campsites at these lakes, crossing the short stream that joins the two. Leaving the forest below, the trail skirts small Heart Lake and reaches barren Selden Pass (10,900 − 2.1). At this pass, many-islanded Marie Lake is the central feature of the view northward, and soon you boulder-hop its clear outlet (10,570 − 0.9), then descend gently to the green expanses of Rosemarie Meadow (10,010 − 1.6). From this grassland a trail forks left, soon climbing southwest to Rose Lake, and about one-fourth mile beyond another trail departs east for Lou Beverly Lake. Both these lakes provide good, secluded camping. About 200 yards past the last junction we bridge West Fork Bear Creek, and then we make a one-mile descent in lodgepole forest to a boulder ford of Bear Creek.

14

15

Marie Lake from Selden Pass

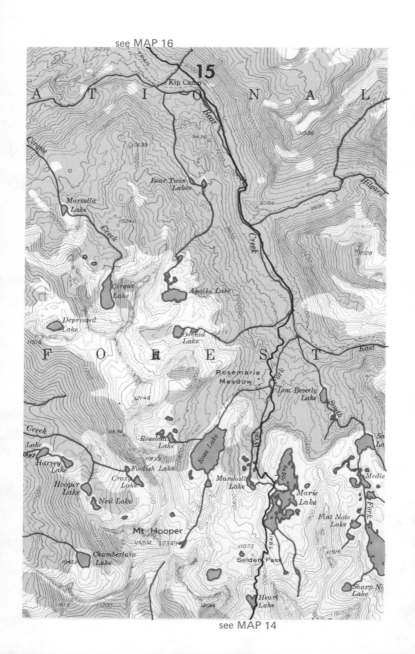

15

Kip Camp

N A T I O N A L

F O R E S T

Cirque
Creek

Marcella
Lake

Bear Twin
Lakes

Bear

Creek

Hilgard

Cirque
Lake

Apollo Lake

Depressed
Lake

Orchid
Lake

Rosemarie
Meadow

East

Lou Beverly
Lake

South

Creek
Lake

Harvey
Lake

Rosebud
Lake

Foolish Lake

Rose Lake

Marshall
Lake

West
Fork

Marie
Lake

Medle

Hooper
Lake

Crazy
Lake

Neil Lake

Flat Note
Lake

Mt. Hooper
VABM 12349

Selden Pass

TRAIL

Fork

Chamberlain
Lake

Sharp N
Lake

Heart
Lake

On the creek's far bank you meet a trail (9350 — 1.4) that goes up East Fork Bear Creek, but you turn down-canyon and descend gently to the log ford of refreshing Hilgard Creek. Immediately beyond, the Lake Italy Trail (9300 — 1.2) climbs to the east, and our trail continues down through the mixed forest cover, always staying near rollicking Bear Creek. You pass many campsites near the trail, but for more wood and more solitude it is better to find a place to camp across the creek. Below Hilgard Creek, where the old trail veered west, we begin (9040 — 2.0) a new trail segment that bypasses the former site of Kip Camp. (If you want to go to Mono Hot Springs for mail, the trail to the left here is one of the trails you might take.) This new segment gradually veers west as it follows the contour line, then turns north at the foot of a tough series of switchbacks. The south-facing hillside here gets plenty of sun, but it is surprisingly wet even in late season, so that you can pleasure your eyes with flowers in bloom and pleasure your throat with cold draughts. Your route then levels off, and at the crest of Bear Ridge passes a trail (9980 — 1.6) that descends to the road to Mono Hot Springs.

15

16

The north side of Bear Ridge is incised with 53 switchbacks, which began in pure lodgepole forest but successively penetrate the realms of mountain hemlock, silver pine, red fir, Jeffrey pine, aspen, white fir and, finally, cottonwoods at Mono Creek (7750 — 4.6). Campsites lie several hundred yards west down the trail after you cross the bridge over the creek, and Vermilion Valley resort is six miles down this trail. Beyond the bridge, the John Muir Trail turns right, soon crosses North Fork Mono Creek, and climbs to a junction with the Mono Pass Trail (8270 — 1.6). Your steep trail levels briefly at lush Pocket Meadow (good campsites), fords North Fork Mono Creek on a log (8940 — 1.4) and then resumes climbing as the route

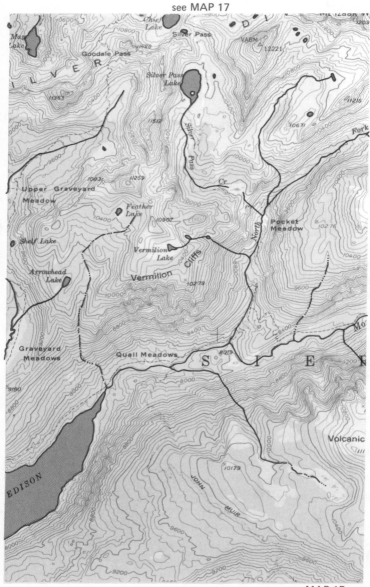

turns up the west canyon wall. From here to Silver Pass the trail was extensively rerouted and overly constructed in 1980-81.

The first ford of Silver Pass, on this wall, may be difficult in early season, and a slip there could be fatal. Above a large meadow we reford the creek (9640 — 1.2) and then rise above timberline. The new trail bypasses Silver Pass Lake and then ascends past the actual pass (low point) to the sign *Silver Pass* (10,900 — 2.8) at a glorious viewpoint on the Silver Divide. The descent northward passes Chief Lake and then the Goodale Pass Trail (10,550 — 1.2), switchbacks northeast down to ford the small outlet of Squaw Lake, and then makes a long, hemlock-lined descent to the beautiful valley of Fish Creek, where there are good campsites near the junction with the Cascade Valley Trail (9130 — 2.5). Turning right here, you ascend northeast and soon cross Fish Creek on a steel bridge. Staying above this good-sized creek, the route ascends gently to the campsites at Tully Hole (9520 — 1.1), a well-flowered grassland where the McGee Pass Trail departs east-

16

17

Tully Hole

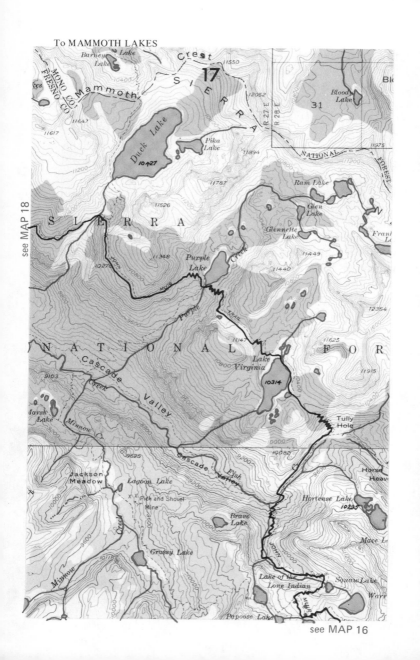

To MAMMOTH LAKES

see MAP 18

see MAP 16

Lake Virginia

ward. Now the John Muir Trail climbs steeply north up a band of Mesozoic metavolcanics which sweep east and grade into the Paleozoic metasediments of dominating Red Slate Mountain (13,163'). Beyond the crest of this ascent you reach deep-blue Lake Virginia (10,314 − 1.9), with several somewhat exposed campsites. In early season you will have to wade across the head of the lake or detour rather far north. From this boggy crossing your trail climbs to a saddle below the vertical northeast face of Peak 11147 and then switchbacks down to heavily used Purple Lake (9900 − 2.1), at whose outlet a trail begins its descent into deep Cascade Valley.

17

From Purple Lake the rocky trail climbs west and then bends north as it levels out high on the wall of glaciated Cascade Valley. Soon you pass a trail to Duck Lake (10,150 − 2.3), and just beyond it ford Duck Creek, near several undistinguished campsites. During dry seasons, fill your canteen in Duck Creek, as the next water is at Deer Creek, six mile ahead. From this ford the John Muir Trail contours southwest, and then slants northwest as it descends through mixed conifers. If you sharpen your gaze, you will see both red firs and Jeffrey pines above 10,000 feet on this north wall of Cascade Valley, well above their normal range. You also have fine views of the Silver Divide in the south as you slant northwest and descend gradually through mixed conifers. Then the trail bends northeast, drops to cross Deer Creek (9120 − 5.8) amid some fair campsites, and leads

18

north through a long meadow overseen by The Thumb (10,286′). Beyond a seasonal stream you meet a trail

19

to Mammoth Pass (8920 − 2.2) in Upper Crater Meadow. At the far end of this meadow the old John Muir/Pacific Crest Trail goes straight ahead, but the new trail veers slightly left to descend a ravine that contains Crater Creek, which we soon ford. Then we look down on expansive Crater Meadow, and beyond it see hulking Mammoth Mountian, with its barren upper slopes and a garish building on top. On this mountain's north slopes as many as 20,000 skiers, most of them from southern California, may be found on a busy day. This mountain erupted and began to grow about 400,000 years ago, and the erupted material eventually piled up higher than the height of the mountain today. The area around Mammoth Mountain, including the upper canyon of Middle Fork San Joaquin River, has been volcanically active for the last three million years, and the last eruption here occurred less than 1000 years ago. It is the Sierra's "hot spot"—ironically, considering that it is also a mecca for skiers due to its large snowpack.

After fording Crater Creek at the foot of the meadow (8700 − 0.9), in the shadow of the Red Cones, our route descends for 2/3 mile to a hairpin turn over looking an unmapped creek. Several switchbacks later, we curve around a dramatic pond that is the source of the southernmost of four branches of Boundary Creek. Here the gradient lessens consider-

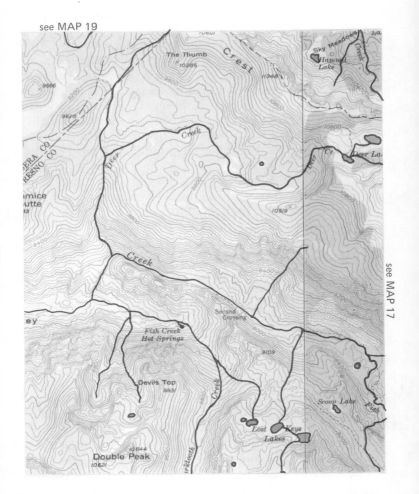

ably, and we hop or log-cross the branches. Less than a mile beyond we come to a road on our right which leads ½ mile north to Reds Meadow Resort, where you can get supplies, meals and showers. Nearby you can shower in the naturally heated waters of Reds Meadow Hot Springs. About 300 yards farther on is another dirt road to the resort, and 250 yards beyond

19

that is a trail north to the resort and south to Fish Creek. Just beyond it is another trail south to Rainbow Falls and Fish Creek and a road-trail north to a parking lot near Reds Meadow Resort. In ½ mile from this junction we reach another, where a trail leads north to Devils Postpile and south to Rainbow Falls. Just beyond, to the west, this new PCT segment crosses Middle Fork San Joaquin River on a sturdy wooden bridge (7400 — 3.6).

From the bridge we pass several ponds and then ascend the west wall of the river canyon on a dusty path that passes the left-branching King Creek Trail. From spots on this west wall we have views of the large meadow near Devils Postpile and of the monumental Postpile itself. The old PCT/John Muir route went directly past this monument, and one may wonder whether the new detour is really the best course. While traveling momentarily east we reach a junction where the PCT continues levelly north but our Muir Trail veers left, uphill, and climbs past the Beck Lakes Trail junction to Minaret Creek. Here we cross this swirling stream on logs and hike one-fourth mile to boggy Johnston Meadow (8120 — 2.0), from where the Minaret Lake Trail continues northwest but our route climbs east, then north toward the lake-dotted slopes of Volcanic Ridge, high above the Middle Fork. The first lake you encounter here is lower Trinity Lake (9180 — 2.0), a shallow, pleasant lake set in silver and lodgepole pines. After passing the other, strung-out ponds and lakelets of the Trinity Lakes, the trail goes through a saddle and drops to hemlock-fringed little Gladys Lake (9580 — 1.8), also with good campsites. A few minutes beyond you descend to skirt round Rosalie Lake (9350 — 0.6), with more good camps. Then the trail makes 20 switchbacks down a cool, north-facing slope that offers frequent tree-framed views of those twin

Devils Postpile   *Jeffrey P. Schaffer*

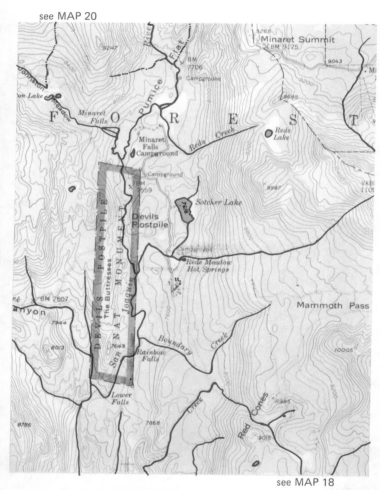

see MAP 18

metamorphic monuments, Mt. Ritter (13,157′) and Banner Peak (12,945′). At the bottom of this descent is beautiful Shadow Lake, a classic case of chronic congestion that may have to be declared off limits for a while. You should camp elsewhere even it it isn't. Immediately beyond a bridge over Shadow Creek you meet a trail (8750 − 1.5) going east down

20

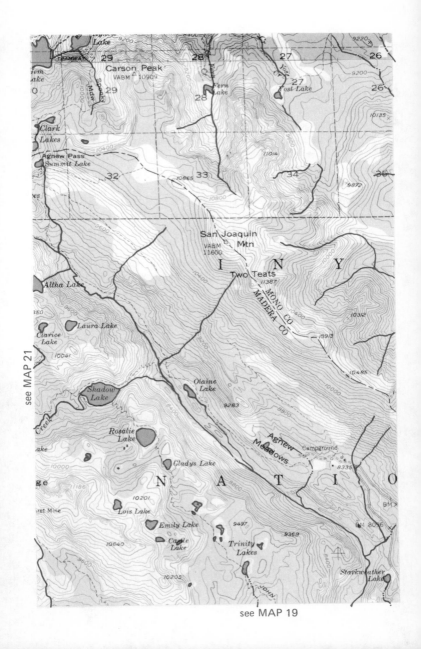

see MAP 21

see MAP 19

to Agnew Meadows, and turn west up the canyon, passing many well-used campsites.

Soon your route turns north at the Ediza Lake **20** Trail junction (9030 − 1.1) and climbs a respectable **21** 1000 feet to timberline, fording a small unnamed creek twice. A swimming-pool-sized pond at the saddle atop this ascent warms up enough in midsummer for pleasant bathing. Then the trail switchbacks down to the many poor-to-fair campsites around windy Garnet Lake, passing a trail down to Middle Fork San Joaquin River at the outlet (9680 − 2.4). More switchbacks configure the very rocky trail that climbs north from Garnet Lake to a ridgetop where Ruby Lake and Emerald Lake offer fair-to-good camping and sweeping, dramatic views of the somber Ritter Range in the west and the low Sierra crest in the east. Then once more our rollercoaster trail descends, to reach the outlet of more-or-less correctly named 1000 Island Lake and, just beyond, a junction (9834 − 2.0) with a trail that leads southeast as far as Agnew Meadows. This lake has many usually windy

Shadow Lake

campsites, and excellent views of Banner Peak, memorialized in some of Ansel Adams' most often seen photographs.

From this junction our route climbs up an easy ridge, utilizing one switchback, and levels off through lodgepole and hemlock trees to reach the meadows and ponds of Island Pass (10,200 − 1.8), where you could camp in early season when there is still flowing water. From here you descend northwest to Rush Creek Forks. Along the one-fourth-mile trail segment before a junction with the Rush Creek Trail (9600 − 1.5) the early-season hiker will have at least three wet fords to make—then keep your boots off till you finally reach the junction. In the Forks area, small camps abound, virtually all of them illegal since they are within 100 feet of a creek or trail. A seasonal

21

Ritter and Banner over Garnet Lake

19

30

31

Gem Lake
8052

Billy Lake

Rush

Waugh Lake
9424

Waugh Lake

Rush Creek

Weber Lake
10508

Sullivan Lake

Island Pass
10492

10587

10474

Thousand Island Lake

JOHN

MUIR

Emerald Lake

Ruby Lake

Badger Lake

9834

10572

10365

11501

Davis

10000

Garnet Lake

10324

TRAIL

Lake Catherine
11034

11158

Banner Peak
12945

10736

10704

Mt Ritter
13157

Nydiver Lakes

Shadow

Cabin L.

Ediza Lake

Volcanic

Rid

11246

11501

12344

Iceberg Lake

Cecile Lake

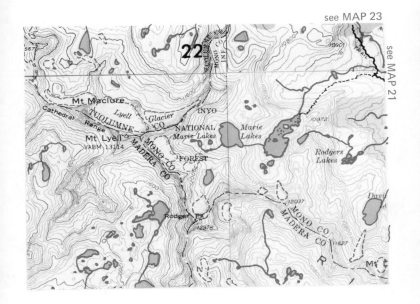

ranger stationed 5 miles east below Waugh Lake may drop by to enforce the rules. In any event, you will find greater solitude if you avoid the overused camping spots at the Forks. You might also have a little less problem with bears, for they tend to investigate the most-used areas first.

Leaving the Forks, we quickly engage some short, steep switchbacks that we follow northwest up to a ridge, then cross it and ease up to a junction with the Marie Lakes Trail (10,030 − 0.8). The lakes' outlet creek, just beyond the junction, is best crossed at an obvious jump-across spot slightly downstream. After the ford our trail winds excessively in an oft-futile attempt to avoid the boulders and bogs of the increasingly alpine environment. Whitebark pines diminish in number and stature as you climb toward a conspicuous saddle—easily mistaken in early season for

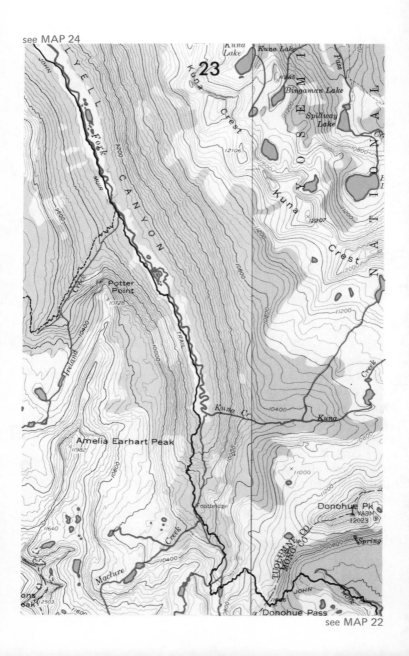

23

Kuna Lake

Kuna Lake

EMI

Bingaman Lake

Spillway Lake

Kuna Crest

12106

Kuna Crest

12207

JOHN

Muir

LYELL FORK CANYON

9200

9600

Ireland Creek

Potter Point

10728

10400

TRAIL

10000

10800

11200

Amelia Earhart Peak
11982

10800

Kuna Cr.

10400

Kuna

11000

11200

10800

Creek

Footbridge

Donohue PK
VABM
12023

Spring

11640

Macure Creek

10400

TUOLUMNE CO
MONO CO

10800

11646

JOHN

Muir

Donohue Pass

Donohue Pass. After a wet slog across the tundra-and-stone floor of our alpine basin, we veer southwest toward a prominent peak and ascend a sometimes obscure trail past blocks and over slabs to the real, signed, tarn-blessed Donohue Pass (11,056 − 3.0).

22

23

The Yosemite high country unfolds before us as we descend northwest, partly in a long, straight fracture (southbound hikers take note). We then curve west to a sharp bend southeast, a few yards from which we can get a commanding panorama of Mt. Lyell, at 13,144 feet Yosemite's highest peak, and deep Lyell Canyon. Leaving the bend, we now descend southwest one-half mile to the north end of a boulder-dotted tarn that occasionally reflects Lyell and its broad glacier—the largest one to be seen from the Muir Trail. Here a tantalizing trail starts north, but this route down large talus blocks should not be attempted with a heavy pack. Rather, contour along the tarn's west shore, then briefly climb southeast to a gap in a low ridge. Next, wind north and soon begin a steep northeast descent that ends at the north end of a small meadow, where you ford the Lyell headwaters (10,220 − 1.8). Among the whitebark pines in this area you'll find the first adequate campsites since the Rush Creek Forks.

Upper Lyell Base Camp

Larger campsites appear on a forested bench by another Lyell Fork crossing (9700 − 1.8). Now we'll stay on the west bank of the river all the way to Tuolumne Meadows. Beyond the bench we make our last major descent—a steep one—down to the Lyell Fork base camp (9000 − 1.4), at the southern, upper end of Lyell Canyon. This camp, a three-hour trek from Highway 120, is a popular site with weekend mountaineers. Our hike to the highway is now an easy, level, usually open stroll along meandering Lyell

23 Fork. A major camping area is found at the junction (8800 − 2.8) with a trail to Vogelsang High Sierra Camp. Note that some of these campsites have steel cables strung between trees. On these cables you can hang a bag of food, counterbalanced at the other end of your short rope by a rock or other weight.

Past the junction, occasional backward glances at receding Potter Point mark your progress north along trout-inhabited Lyell Fork. With the oft-looming threat of afternoon lightning storms, one wishes the trail would have been routed along the forest's edge, rather than through open meadow. Typical of meadowy trails, ours is multitracked. Numerous tracks

Mt. Lyell at head of Lyell Canyon

see MAP 25
see MAP 23

arise mainly because as the main track is used, it gets deepened until it penetrates the near-surface water table and becomes soggy. Odds are great that you'll have to leave the track at least once, thus helping to start a new one.

Shortly after Potter Point finally disappears from view—and beyond half a dozen campsites—we curve northwest, descend between two bedrock outcrops, and then contour west through alternating soggy meadows and lodgepole forests. Both abound in mosquitoes through late July, as does most of the Tuolumne Meadows area. Two-branched Rafferty Creek soon appears, its second branch being a wet ford in early season. Just beyond it we meet the Rafferty Creek Trail (8710 − 4.4), part of the very scenic and very popular High Sierra Loop Trail. We continue west and soon meet another junction (8650 − 0.7), from where a trail goes three-fourths mile west to a junction immediately east of the Tuolumne Meadows Campground. (From there, the left branch skirts around the camp's south perimeter to rejoin the John Muir Trail 2-1/3 miles from our spot, while the right branch quickly ends at the camp's main road. This road leads one-half mile west to Highway 120, and just southwest on it you'll find services.)

Most Muir Trail hikers stop in Tuolumne Meadows, staying at the campground or even at the lodge, and catch a ride, if they can, to the Budd Creek trailhead, about 1½ miles west of the store on Highway 120. But purists who want to do the *entire* John Muir Trail will need the following description of how to stay on the JMT from the junction three-fourths mile east of the campground.

After turning north at this junction, you soon come to a pair of bridges across the Lyell Fork. A photographing pause here is well worth it, particularly when clouds are building up over Mts. Dana and Gibbs in the northeast. From the bridges, a short, winding climb north followed by an equal descent brings us to the Dana Fork of the Tuolumne River, only 20 yards past a junction with an east-climbing trail to the Gaylor Lakes. Immediately beyond the crossing we meet (8690 − 0.6) a short spur trail northeast to the Tuolumne Meadows Lodge. Here you'll find both showers and meals, but on busy weekends you must make dinner reservations early in the day.

The Muir Trail parallels the Dana Fork downstream, encountering a second spur trail northeast to the lodge. Soon you hear the stream as it makes a small drop into a clear pool, which is almost cut in two by a protruding granite finger. At the base of this finger, about 8 to 10 feet down, is an underwater arch—an extremely rare feature in any kind of rock. If you feel like braving the cold water, 50° at best, you can dive under and swim through it. Just beyond the pool, we approach the lodge's road (8650

— 0.3), where a short path climbs a few yards up to it and takes one to the entrance of a large parking lot for backpackers. Now we parallel the paved road westward, passing the Tuolumne Meadows Ranger Station and quickly reaching a junction. The main road curves north to the sometimes-noisy highway, but we follow the spur road west, to where it curves into a second large parking lot for backpackers. In its east end you'll find a booth from which a summer ranger dispenses wilderness permits. Our road past the lot becomes a closed dirt road and diminishes to a wide trail by the time we arrive at Highway 120 (8595 — 0.8). A store and post office lie on the highway just southwest of the Tuolumne River bridge, and a visitor center is a mile to the west.

24

The Muir route crosses the highway, passes another parking lot, and follows a dirt road one-third mile west to a gate that blocks cars from proceeding farther. Past the gate, we continue west along the lodgepole-dotted flank of Tuolumne Meadows, enjoying fine views south across the meadows to Unicorn Peak,

Soda Springs

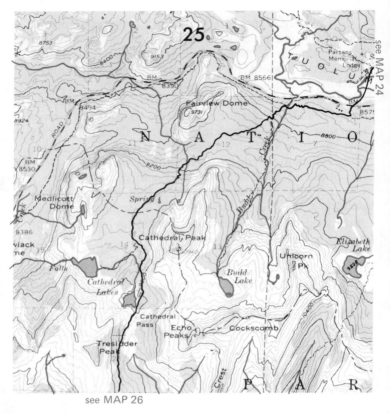

see MAP 26

see MAP 24

24

25

Cathedral Peak and some of the knobby Echo Peaks. Coming to a road fork (8590 − 0.7), we bear left through an old parking loop and across a bridge over the Tuolumne River. Then we stroll southwest across the expansive meadows to another highway crossing (8575 − 0.5) and beyond the blacktop ascend gently for 300 yards to a junction with the Tenaya Lake/ Tuolumne Meadows Trail. The Muir route turns right on this wide, dusty trail, and proceeds west for three-fourths mile in thick lodgepole forest. Then it crosses rippling Budd Creek on a sturdy bridge and immedately meets the Cathedral Lakes Trail (8570 − 1.1), which begins at a parking lot beside the highway (the Budd Creek trailhead) a few steps north of here. Turning left onto this trail, we begin to climb steeply.

After three-fourths mile of taxing ascent under a welcome forest cover, the dusty trail levels off and descends to a small meadow that is boggy in early season. From here we can see the dramatically shaped tops of Unicorn Peak and The Cockscomb. The apparent granite dome in the south is in reality the north ridge of Cathedral Peak, whose steeples are out of sight over the "dome's" horizon.

Our viewful trail continues to cruise gently up and down through more little meadows set in hemlock forest, and then dips near a tinkling stream whose source, we discover after further walking, is a robust spring on a shady set of switchbacks. Beyond this climb our tread levels off on the west slope of Cathedral Peak and makes a long, gentle, sparsely forested descent on sandy underfooting to a junction (9460 − 2.7) with the spur trail to lower Cathedral Lake.

25

Many hikers wanting to camp soon follow this spur trail two-thirds mile down to the lake's bedrock east shore. A rust-stained waterline on the meadow side of the bedrock marks the high-water level when the meadow floods in early season. (The iron for the rust is derived from the meadow's soil, not from the iron-deficient granitic bedrock.) Campsites abound on both the north and south shores, the northern ones being roomier. As do all popular Yosemite lakes, this one attracts black bears.

Perhaps after a swim in its relatively warm waters, return to the John Muir Trail and make an easy mile-long climb to the southeast corner of very shallow upper Cathedral Lake. Although camping is wisely prohibited here, you may enjoy a stop for a snack on the south-shore peninsula, from which you can at times get good mirrored-image photos of two-steepled Cathedral Peak. Our trail then climbs one-fourth mile to broad Cathedral Pass (9730 − 1.1), where the excellent views include Tresidder Peak, Cathedral Peak, Echo Peaks, Matthes Crest, the Clark Range farther south, and Matterhorn Peak far to the north.

Beyond the pass is a long, beautiful swale, the headwaters of Echo Creek, where the midseason flower show is worth the hike from Tuolumne Meadows. Our path traverses up the east flank of Tresidder Peak on a gentle climb to the actual high point of this trail segment, at a marvelous viewpoint overlooking most of southern Yosemite Park. The inspiring panorama includes the peaks around Vogelsang High Sierra Camp in the southeast, the whole Clark Range in the south, and the peaks on the Park border in both directions farther away. From this viewpoint our high trail traverses under steep-walled Columbia Finger, then switchbacks quickly down to the head of the upper lobe of Long Meadow, levels off, and leads down a gradually sloping valley dotted with little lodgepole pines to the head of the second, lower lobe of l-o-n-g Long Meadow. After passing a junction (9340 − 2.7) with a trail down Echo Creek, the route levels off and heads south one-half mile before bending west one-fourth mile to pass below Sunrise High Sierra Camp (9340 − 0.8), perched on a granite bench just above the trail. South of the camp are some backpacker campsites from where you can take in the next morning's glorious sunrise.

The trail continues through the south arm of Long Meadow, then soon starts to climb the eastern slopes of Sunrise Mountain. You top a broad southeast-trending ridge, and then, paralleling the headwaters of Sunrise Creek, descend steeply by switchbacks down a rocky canyon. At the foot of this descent you cross a trickling creek, then climb a low moraine to another

see MAP 27

26

Mildred Lake

Columbia Finger

Echo Lake

Matthes Lake

Sunrise Lakes

Sunrise Camp

Sunrise Mtn

Kuna Lake

Babcock Lake

Echo Valley

Merced Lake

High Sierra Campground

Merced Ranger

Footbridge

Footbridge

RIVER

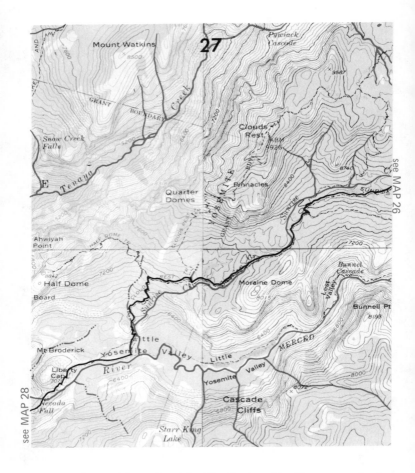

see MAP 26

see MAP 28

26

creek, and in a short half mile top the linear crest of a giant lateral moraine. This moraine is the largest of a series of ridgelike glacial deposits in this area, and the gigantic granite boulders along their sides testify to the power of the glacier that once filled Little Yosemite Valley and its tributary valleys. Most of its rocks have decomposed to soil—an indication of its old age. More morainal crests are identified on both sides of the trail and Half Dome is seen through the trees before our trail reaches a junction (8000 − 5.0) with the Forsyth Trail. There are fair campsites on Sunrise Creek about 150 yards north of this junction.

Here we turn south and in a moment reach the High Trail coming in on the left. Turning right, we descend southwest, as our path is bounded on the north by giant cliffs—the south buttress of the Clouds Rest eminence—and on the south by Moraine Dome. **26**

A mile from the last junction the John Muir Trail fords Sunrise Creek in a red-fir forest whose stillness **27** is broken by the creek's gurgling and by the occasional screams of Steller jays. In three-fourths mile we see a good campsite on a large, creekside, shady flat, then

The overhang on Half Dome

Jason Winnett

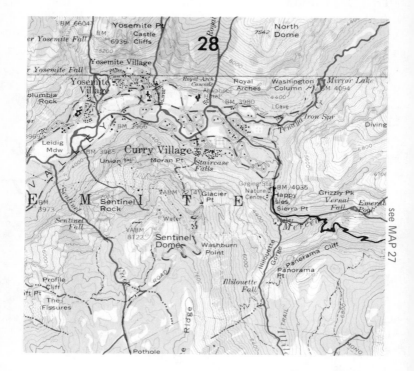

curve northeast to a quick crossing of a tributary which has two west-bank campsites. Immediately past them is a trail to Clouds Rest (7210 − 2.3) and one-half mile west from this junction we meet the trail to Half Dome (7015 − 0.5)—about four miles round trip, and an incredible hike that shouldn't be missed. From this junction our shady path switchbacks down through a changing forest cover that comes to include some stately incense-cedars, with their burnt-orange, fibrous bark, plus sugar and ponderosa pines, white firs and black oaks. At the foot of this descent a gravelly shortcut trail to the Merced Lake Trail goes southwest, and its extension northeast ends in 100 yards at some improved campsites on Sunrise Creek.

Vernal and Nevada falls from Glacier Point

We continue straight ahead 350 yards across the flat floor of Little Yosemite Valley to a junction (6120 − 1.5) with the Merced Lake Trail, close beside the green pools of the lovely river. A summer ranger usually camps just east of this junction, in the heart of bear country. Turning right, we pass numerous campsites and then ascend almost imperceptibly over a little rise that marks the west end of Little Yosemite Valley. Beyond it, we soon reach a junction with a foot trail to Happy Isles which is more scenic than the slightly longer John Muir Trail segment down to Happy Isles. Then, in one-fourth mile we are at the

27

top of Nevada Fall. Here the Merced River takes its mightiest plunge—594 feet. The view from the brink of the fall is unforgettable—the cauldron of flying water stands in stark relief to the serenity of the trail, and the barren solidity of Liberty Cap is a reassuring reminder of the solid rock on which the viewer stands.

27   About 300 yards beyond the fall, the Panorama Trail (5950 − 1.4) departs southward, bound for Glacier Point, and the Muir Trail follows a paved,
28   walled-in section that clings to the side of a very steep granite slope. Then it switchbacks down to Clark Point (5481 − 1.0), where there are fine views of the deep canyon of the Merced River and its great falls. From here a lateral trail switchbacks quickly down to Emerald Pool, a favorite, though potentially dangerous, swimming hole used by Park employees and visitors alike. From this vantage point your trail descends steeply by a score of switchbacks on an asphalt tread, down to a wooden bridge (4520 − 1.1) over the river from which a million photographs of Vernal Fall have been taken. Then the trail rises briefly onto the steep north canyon wall, curves down around Sierra Point while staying high above the cascading river, and finally descends past minor trail junctions to the end of the John Muir Trail by a stream-gaging station at Happy Isles (4035 − 0.9). Here you can catch a free shuttle bus to Yosemite Valley points, or you can hike one last mile on trail to Camp Curry.

Muir Trail Southbound

For some reason or other, you may want to walk south on the Muir Trail. So that you can avoid "reading the description backward," here is a brief description of the trail as it would appear to the southbound hiker.

See the description in Chapter 3 for the locations of summer ranger stations, and for special rules applying to particular areas. (In the following description, an asterisk means "this ford is difficult in early season.")

From Happy Isles (4035 — 0.0) in Yosemite Valley, the John Muir Trail begins as an asphalt ribbon that climbs the wall of the spectacular Merced River canyon. It has been asphalted because it is so heavily used. Perhaps 50% of the people who can say, "I walked on the John Muir Trail" did all their walking within 2 miles of Happy Isles, out of a total of 210 miles. After dipping to cross the Merced River on a wooden bridge, the trail climbs via many switchbacks to viewpoints overlooking Vernal and Nevada Falls and the great granite domes above them. Just before the lip of roaring Nevada Fall (6100 — 4.6) the tough climb ends, and you enter forested Little Yosemite Valley, where camping is fine as long as you bear-proof your food.

After a stroll near the river you reach a junction (6120 — 1.2) where you turn left away from the stream and begin the long ascent to Tuolumne Meadows. Rising through mixed conifers, you reach the trail to the Half Dome (7015 — 1.5)—about four miles round trip, and an incredible hike that shouldn't be missed. Soon we pass the trail to Clouds Rest and jump a little stream. Then, ascending near gurgling Sunrise Creek, we pass first the High Trail to Merced **27** Lake and almost immediately the Forsyth Trail (8000—2.8) to Tenaya Lake. The gentle climbing near **26** Sunrise Creek reaches a boulder ford of the stream, and then you must climb stiffly northeast before you descend to the lower end of Long Meadow and pass below Sunrise High Sierra Camp (9340 — 5.0). There are backpacker campsites just south of this tent-top concession.

Beyond the Echo Creek Trail branching right, the John Muir Trail reaches the upper lobe of Long Meadow, then turns northeast and ascends the slopes **25** below digital Columbia Finger. At the highest trail point between Yosemite Valley and Tuolumne Meadows is a viewpoint with excellent panoramas of the southeast part of the Park. Then the trail descends gently to the flower-filled swale at the south side of Cathedral Pass (9730 — 3.5). From the excellent views at this pass, dominated by steepled Cathedral Peak, you descend past the southeast shore of shallow Upper Cathedral Lake (no camping) and then walk a rocky trail to the junction of a spur path to Lower Cathedral Lake (9460 — 1.1)(camping allowed.)

From the junction a long, gentle ascent on sandy underfooting levels off on the west slope of dominating Cathedral Peak. Then our trail drops down a shady north slope through several delightful, small meadows rimmed with mountain hemlocks. Finally, a dusty, eroded section of trail leads rather steeply down to a junction (8570 — 2.7) near Highway 120 in Tuolumne Meadows.

Most hikers will continue to the highway and then walk east beside it or will catch a ride to the small bit of civilization 1¼ miles east of the trailhead on Highway 120, and then resume hiking on the Muir Trail

east of the public campground or the Tuolumne
Lodge. But purists who are doing the *whole* Muir
Trail will turn right at the last-mentioned junction
and follow the level trail that leads through the forest
south of the highway for ¾ mile to another junction.
After turning left here, you cross the highway in 300
yards and then stroll across open meadows ½ mile to
a bridge over the Tuolumne River. Across the bridge
is an old parking loop, and we take the dirt road that
goes east from it. Soon this road passes through a gate
and then reaches Highway 120 (8595 − 2.3) just east
of the highway bridge.

25

24

You cross the highway and continue on a wide
trail that soon becomes a closed-off dirt road. Then
you pass, on the left, a backpackers' parking lot
which contains a kiosk where wilderness permits are
issued. Now the Muir Trail leads east just south of a
blacktop road that ends at Tuolumne Meadows
Lodge. Just 0.8 mile from the highway, and just be-

The Unicorn over Tuolumne Meadows

fore reaching a second backpackers' parking lot, you
veer southeast away from the road to parallel the
Dana Fork of the Tuolumne River 0.3 miles to a log
bridge over it near the lodge. Beyond this crossing
you turn south, rise over a slight crest and descend to
a bridge over the Lyell Fork of the Tuolumne River.
Not far beyond the stream, the Muir Trail meets a
trail (8650 — 1.7) that hikers re-beginning from the
main campground would be coming up.

Altogether now, we amble eastward past the Rafferty Creek Trail, cross Rafferty Creek*, and then
24 bend southward as we enter the marvelous canyon of
the Lyell Fork. Easy strolling with expansive views
23 leads past a second route to Vogelsang Camp (8800
— 5.1), across Ireland Creek, and on up the canyon to
the Lyell Fork base camp (9000 — 2.8), at the head of
the nearly level wide portion of Lyell Canyon. From
these well-used campsites you climb steeply up the
canyon, crossing the stream on a bridge halfway to
upper Lyell base camp (10,220 — 3.6).

At the camp you ford the river and start climbing
again. Soon you have excellent views of Mt. Lyell,
highest peak in Yosemite, and the large glacier that
clings to its north slope. The trail swings northeast,
then southeast as it ascends rockily to Donohue Pass,
on Yosemite's border (11,056 — 1.8). Now on the
22 east slope of the Sierra for the first and last time, the
John Muir Trail descends into timber and reaches
21 Rush Creek Forks, a popular camping area around the
junction of a trail east to Silver Lake on the June Lake
loop. Soon reaching Island Pass, you re-enter the
Sierra's western slope and traverse down to the outlet
of 1000 Island Lake (9834 — 7.1), where the perma-
nent PCT heads east bound for Agnew Meadows but
you take the John Muir route southeast over a bare
granite ridge, past Ruby Lake to Garnet Lake (9680
— 2.0), where dark, metamorphic Mt. Ritter and Ban-

ner Peak loom mightily above the lake's west end.

From this lake the Muir Trail switchbacks up a ridge and then drops to the banks of rollicking Shadow Creek, which it parallels down to overused Shadow Lake (8750 − 3.5). Twenty switchbacks are then needed to surmount the cool, north-facing slope east of Shadow Lake to round Rosalie Lake. Beyond, the trail passes hemlock-fringed little Gladys Lake and a number of strung-out ponds and lakelets of the Trinity Lakes group. Now a well-forested descent leads to boggy Johnston Meadow, from which it's a short stroll to refreshing Minaret Creek. Past the log ford* of this stream, our trail plunges down through deep, dusty pumice to intersect a recently built segment of the Pacific Crest Trail, and we turn right onto it. Our trail climbs for a long quarter mile, with frequent views down onto the large meadow along the Middle Fork and, eventually, monumental Devils Postpile. Past the right-branching King Creek Trail our dusty trail winds down a steep hillside to a new wooden bridge over the Middle Fork. Just beyond an unmapped trail, our trail continues eastward under moderate forest cover. In ½ mile we reach another junction, where the left branch leads to a parking lot near Reds Meadow Resort and the right one leads to Rainbow Falls. Continuing eastward, the PCT in 100 yards crosses yet another trail that leads south from the resort area. If you want to visit the resort, this is the best trail to turn left onto. The resort has a modest selection of supplies, a cafe, showers and a few cabins. Nearby you can shower in the naturally heated water of Reds Meadow Hot Springs.

After crossing two more roads, while ascending moderately southeast, you hop across a creek that usually flows all year. About ½ mile later, now on level trail, you come to four branches of Boundary

Creek. Immediately beyond the fords, the trail bends northeast around a dramatic pond. Strolling south again, we begin to get fine views across the Middle Fork. After overlooking Crater Creek at a hairpin turn, the trail swings back northward once more before resuming equatorward travel to reach and ford Crater Creek close under the Red Cones. Ascending

19

beyond, we reford Crater Creek and gradually level off as we approach a junction with the old PCT/JMT

18

just before we reach serene Upper Crater Meadow. Here another trail departs for Mammoth Pass, and then your route threads an unnamed meadow before winding through ghostlike red firs anchored in deep pumice to reach a boulder ford* of Deer Creek (9120 — 3.1). (In dry season, fill your canteen.) Then the trail rises, first northeast and then southeast, to the 10,000-foot contour and follows it for several

17

viewful miles where you can look, across deep Cascade Valley, to the crease drained by Duck Creek. You soon boulder-hop this stream, round a major ridge, and switchback down to the many campsites near the outlet of heavily used Purple Lake (9900 — 8.1).

Now you begin to leave the throngs behind as you climb over a ridge to deep-blue Lake Virginia and then drop steeply to Tully Hole, a well-flowered grassland where the McGee Pass Trail departs eastward. In this meadow you meet splashing Fish Creek, and then follow its descending course for a mile before crossing it on a steel bridge. Almost immediately the Muir Trail leaves the creekside and ascends through hemlock-and-fir forest to timberline at Squaw Lake, then

16

climbs steeply above the trees to Silver Pass (10,900 — 8.9)

South of this elegant viewpoint, we pass royal-blue Silver Pass Lake and then ford Silver Pass Creek twice, the second ford* being at the head of a fatally high cascade which demands caution in crossing. At

the foot of the canyon wall you ford North Fork
Mono Creek* and turn south down the creek past
Pocket Meadow to meet the Mono Pass Trail (8270
— 5.2) just beyond another ford* of the North Fork.
In 1½ miles you turn left away from the creekside
trail, which in 6 miles arrives at Vermilion Valley. After crossing Mono Creek on a steel bridge, you climb
long and steadily up Bear Ridge via 53 switchbacks to
a junction (9980 — 4.6) with a trail that leads west to
Mono Hot Springs.

The descent on the south side of Bear Ridge is hot
but wet, with plenty of drinking water. Near the foot,
we pass an old segment of the Muir Trail veering **16**
right, and go left along the hillside, bypassing the site
of old Kip Camp. Then we pass the other end of this **15**
abandoned bit of Muir Trail (9040 — 3.0) and soon
reach the east bank of dashing Bear Creek. Strolling
up its canyon, we pass many fine campsites, particularly across the creek, where use is far less. The junction with the Lake Italy trail is immediately followed
by a log crossing* of Hilgard Branch, and in a long
mile we pass a trail up East Fork Bear Creek just before boulder-hopping Bear Creek.* Then the canyon
steepens and the trail rises to cross Bear Creek on a
log bridge in Rosemarie Meadow just before the trail
to Lou Beverly Lake departs eastward and the trail to
Rose Lake departs westward. Now you approach timberline, reaching it at sprawling Marie Lake before
gently ascending to Selden Pass (10,900 — 7.1).

Your south-descending trail now skirts small Heart
Lake and then winds between the two beautiful Sally **14**
Keyes Lakes before passing a faint shortcut down to
Blaney Meadows. On the descent ahead, you jump
across Senger Creek and switchback to a junction
(10,150 — 5.9) with another trail down to Blaney
Meadows. The hot springs there are sufficient reason
to detour by descending this trail to the Florence

Lake Trail, going 100 yards west, and finding an
unsigned trail that leads ¼ mile, south to riverside
campsites. The hot springs and a warmish lake are
150 yards southwest of them.

14
13
From the hillside junction, the Muir Trail diagonals
southeast down to the South Fork San Joaquin River
Trail and leads up the canyon to a junction with the
Piute Creek Trail at the border of Kings Canyon National Park. Beyond the steel bridge here, your trail
ascends past many riverside campsites, crosses the
river on a bridge, passes the junction of the trail up
the South Fork, recrosses on another bridge, and
ascends steeply eastward to beautiful Evolution Valley
(9240 − 8.6). Just before Evolution Meadow you
cross Evolution Creek * and then you jump across several tributaries before climbing out of the valley to
long, emerald Evolution Lake and skirting it to ford
its inlet (10,850 − 7.1). Now above the trees, the trail
passes well-named Sapphire Lake and an unnamed lake,
jumps Evolution Creek again, and visits barren
Wanda Lake and Lake McDermand on the way to Muir
Pass (11,955 − 4.6).

12

11

From the leaky stone hut at the pass, the alpine
trail quickly drops to the inlet of Helen Lake and
then plays leapfrog with the outlet stream. This east
side of Muir Pass is under snow throughout the summer in some years. Reaching timber, your route
parallels Middle Fork Kings River through Big Pete
Meadow and Little Pete Meadow to the Bishop Pass
Trail, leading east (8710 − 7.0). Immediately you
cross vigorous Dusy Branch on a steel bridge and then
follow an easy trail down to lush Grouse Meadows.
Then, beyond a series of falls and chutes in the tum-
bling river, the Muir Trail turns left where the Middle
Fork Trail (8020 − 3.3) continues down to Simpson
Meadow.

10

9

Heading east up the canyon of Palisade Creek, the
trail hops a number of tributaries and then arrives

Lake McDermand and Wanda Lake from Muir Pass

Mt. Goddard over Wanda Lake

at pleasant Deer Meadow. Soon you cross multi-branched Glacier Creek and about ¾ mile later your trail attacks the canyon wall via a trail segment **8** called the Golden Staircase. This steep climb ends where the trail nearly touches the outlet of lower Palisade Lake, and then the route passes high above the two sapphire Palisade Lakes and leaves the trees for an assault on the ramparts of formidable Mather Pass (12,100 − 10.2).

At this pass you begin a long descent that first winds among the ponds and lakelets of desolate **7** Upper Basin, in the morning shadow of dominating Split Mountain. The trail fords several branches of the headwaters of South Fork Kings River, then the young fork itself and finally an unnamed but vigorous stream before it comes to a trail (10,160 − 4.9) heading east to Taboose Pass. In 1/3 mile, where the South Fork Trail leads southwest down the river to the unmaintained Cartridge Pass Trail, you turn left and if you are lucky find a log 100 yards upstream on which to cross the noisy South Fork.* Then the trail climbs to timberline, passes another trail to Taboose Pass, fords the Lake Marjorie outlet stream and meets the trail to Bench Lake. After climbing past four enticing lakelets, you touch the outlet of large Lake **6** Marjorie and then climb vigorously southeast above it to brown-hued Pinchot Pass (12,130 − 4.6).

Beyond the steep slope south of the pass, your trail winds among alpine flower gardens bounded by spectacular peaks on 3½ sides. Then, just beyond the Sawmill Pass Trail junction, the gradient steepens and you descend sharply to Woods Creek, which you parallel past its White Fork* to a bridge crossing (8492 − 7.1) of this creek just below the confluence of its South Fork. Now the trail ascends beside the South Fork, crossing the outlet of Lake 10296 on a wooden bridge and several unnamed tributaries via jumping or

5

rock-hopping. At the outlet of overused but handsome Dollar Lake (10,230 − 3.7) the Baxter Pass Trail leads east and the Muir Trail continues its gentle-to-moderate climb, soon fording South Fork Woods Creek* and skirting above aptly named Arrowhead Lake.

Now you arrive at the justly famous, beautiful Rae Lakes, where Dragon Peak, Mt. Rixford, Painted Lady and Fin Dome make excellent photographic subjects when the light is right. Just beyond the isthmus between the upper two lakes, the 60 Lakes Trail leads west and you tackle the last, hard climb to rockbound Glen Pass (11,978 − 4.6). This side of the pass may be under snow in early season. The steep

Glen Pass

south wall of Glen Pass is easily negotiated on the well-graded trail, and soon you are strolling on the tree-dotted slopes high above emerald Charlotte Lake.

Just ¼ mile beyond a shortcut trail leading left toward Kearsarge Pass, you come to an X junction (10,710 − 2.3) in a broad, sandy saddle, where the Muir Trail diagonals across the trail from Kearsarge Pass to Charlotte Lake. Soon you make a steep descent past the Bullfrog Lake Trail and on down into the wooded valley of Bubbs Creek, where a trail (9550 − 2.2) turns right (west) bound for Cedar Grove.

Turning east, you hike beside large Vidette Meadow under the shadow of the spiring, fracturing Kearsarge Pinnacles. Then you begin to climb toward the *last* (and highest) pass on the Muir Trail, Forester Pass. Staying near splashing Bubbs Creek, you pass a trail to Center Basin (10,500 − 2.8) and ford the basin's outlet stream.* Then you cross and recross the headwaters of Bubbs Creek before swinging high above Lake 12248 and puffing up the switchbacks (snow-covered in early season) to windy Forester Pass (13,180 − 4.5).

The trail on the south side of this pass is cut right into the cliff in places, and a bit of caution is in order, despite the very tempting views before you. Below the headwall, the trail winds among high, rock-bound lakes at the headwaters of the Kern River. Just below the first tree patches, the trail to Lake South America and Milestone Basin departs westward, and about ¾ mile beyond you make a formidable ford* of Tyndall Creek. Immediately across the stream, the Shepherd Pass Trail (10,930 − 5.0) departs northeast, and the Muir Trail begins a rising traverse up the talus-clad west slope of Tawny Point. At the top of this ascent you are on Bighorn Plateau, a marvelous viewpoint almost without equal in the entire High Sierra. Soon a three-stage descent leads to the bould-

ery valley of Wright Creek, which you eventually find
and ford.* An almost level stroll then leads to the lip
of Wallace Creek canyon, where the Kaweah Peaks
stand noble on the southwest horizon. The trail then
quickly drops to a ford* of Wallace Creek (10,390
— 5.6), where the High Sierra Trail starts west toward
Junction Meadow. Beyond this ford your rocky trail
climbs again, reaching a high saddle before descending
past so-called Sandy Meadow. Just over a foxtail-pine-
clad ridge, we meet a junction (10,880 — 3.3) from
where the Pacific Crest Trail continues south toward
Mexico but our Muir Trail turns east to seek its ter-
minus, Mt. Whitney, which soon comes into view.
Our trail through the pine forest then drops to Whitney Creek, which can be boulder-hopped most of the
year, and passes the trail to Crabtree Meadows. Just
beyond is the Crabtree Ranger Station, and in ½ mile
we pass the last campsites before timberline, in a nice
little meadow at the confluence of Whitney Creek
and an unnamed tributary. Ahead, Timberline Lake

2

Between Wright Creek and Wallace Creek

(11,070 – 3.2), though somewhat wooded, is closed to camping.

From this rest stop, we ascend briskly to Guitar Lake, hopping its inlet stream with no difficulty. Then, past an unnamed lakelet, we begin a challenging series of switchbacks, which culminate 1500 feet higher at the junction (13,560 – 4.1) with the Mt. Whitney Trail from Whitney Portal on the east side. Here the Muir Trail turns left, and we cannot help but feel a keen anticipation as we begin the last two miles. As we wind among the large blocks of talus, we often have views, through notch-windows, of Owens Valley, 10,000 feet below us in the east. Finally, we see ahead on an almost level plateau a stone hut near the summit, and with a well-earned feeling of accomplishment we take the last few steps to the highest point in the "lower 48" states (14,495 – 2.0).

The author at Forester Pass

Trail Profiles

Trail profiles help you see trail distance and steepness at a glance. Below is a profile for the Mt. Whitney Trail. The 6 pages after that show the entire John Muir Trail in profile.

In these profiles the vertical scale is greatly exaggerated. One vertical inch equals 1568 feet of elevation, whereas one horizontal inch equals three miles. Nevertheless, the steepness of the slopes on these profiles is related to how you feel when you have to carry a pack up them.

Note that horizontal distance is measured along the horizontal axis, not along the profile line. Hence, the steeper a line segment, the more the distance along it will exceed the actual distance between the points it connects.

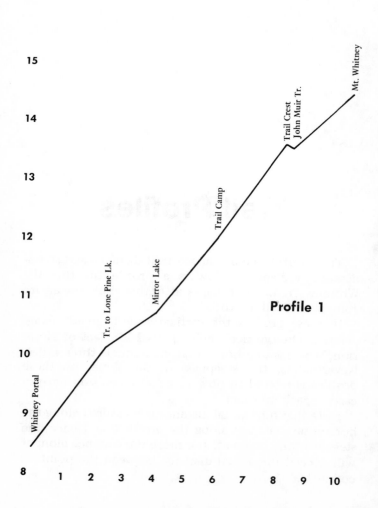

Profile 1

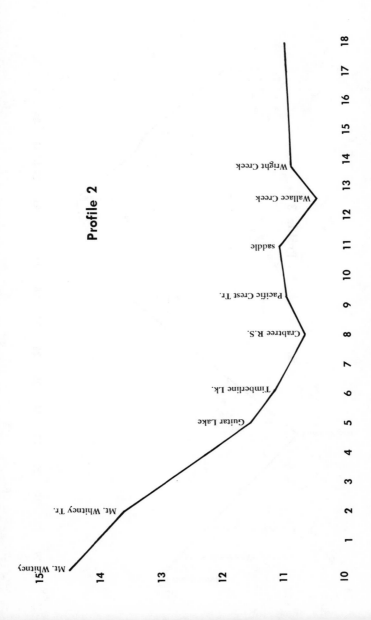

Profile 2

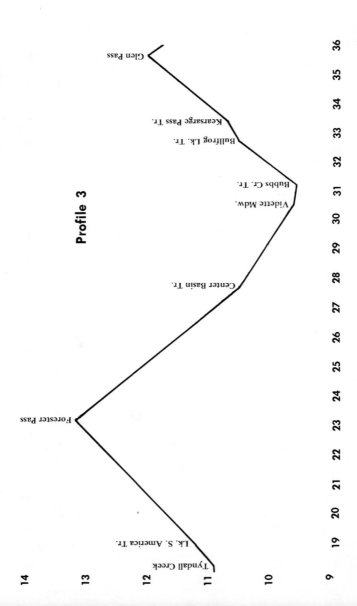

Profile 3

Tyndall Creek
Lk. S. America Tr.
Forester Pass
Center Basin Tr.
Vidette Mdw.
Bubbs Cr. Tr.
Bullfrog Lk. Tr.
Kearsarge Pass Tr.
Glen Pass

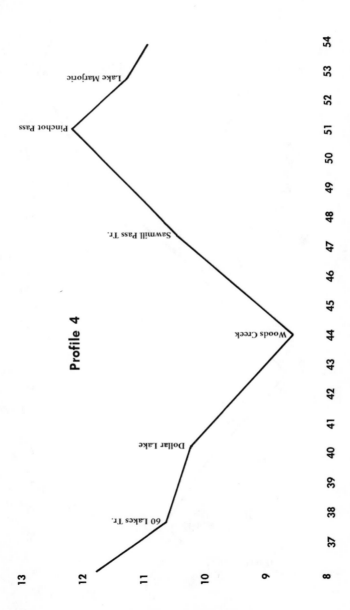

Profile 4

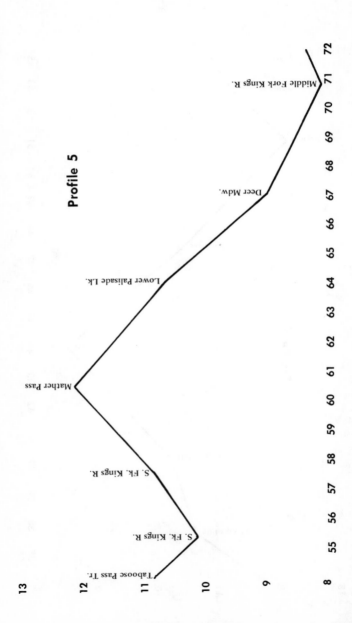

Profile 5

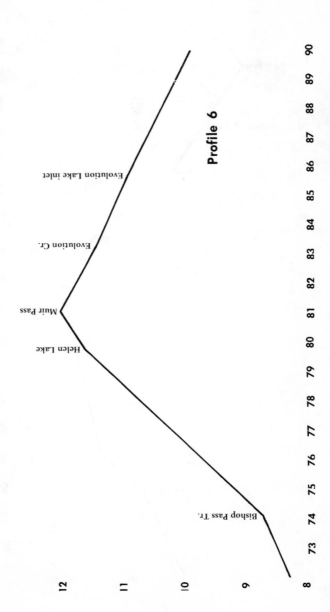

Profile 6

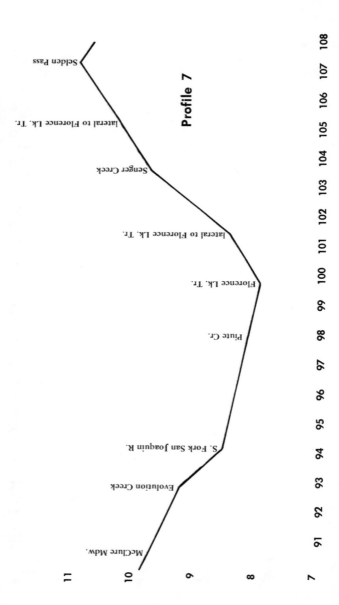

Profile 7

McClure Mdw.
Evolution Creek
S. Fork San Joaquin R.
Piute Cr.
Florence Lk. Tr.
lateral to Florence Lk. Tr.
Senger Creek
lateral to Florence Lk. Tr.
Selden Pass

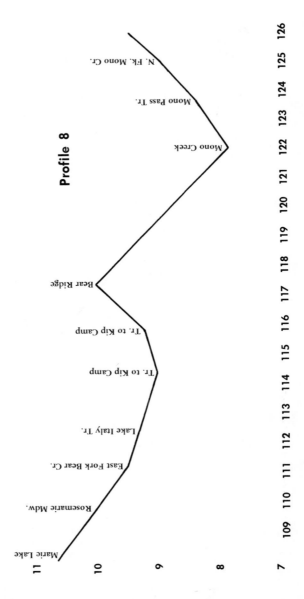

Profile 8

- Marie Lake
- Rosemarie Mdw.
- East Fork Bear Cr.
- Lake Italy Tr.
- Tr. to Kip Camp
- Tr. to Kip Camp
- Bear Ridge
- Mono Creek
- Mono Pass Tr.
- N. Fk. Mono Cr.

Profile 9

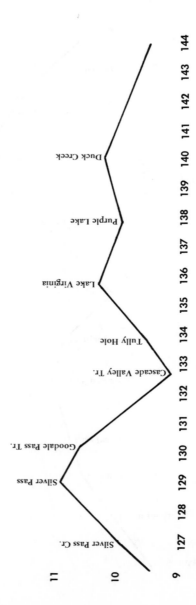

Profile 10

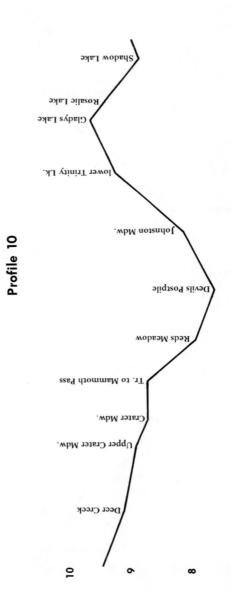

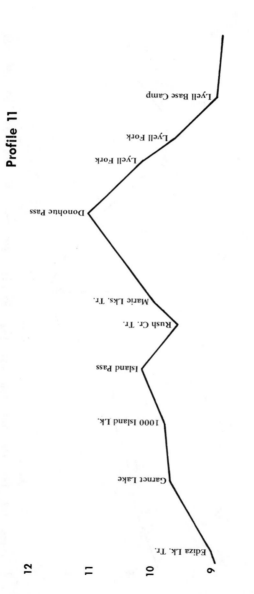

Profile 11

Ediza Lk. Tr.
Garnet Lake
1000 Island Lk.
Island Pass
Rush Cr. Tr.
Marie Lks. Tr.
Donohue Pass
Lyell Fork
Lyell Fork
Lyell Base Camp

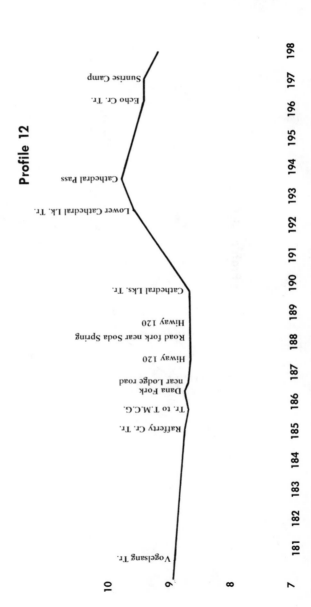

Profile 12

Vogelsang Tr.

Rafferty Cr. Tr.
Tr. to T.M.C.G.
Dana Fork near Lodge road
Hiway 120
Road fork near Soda Spring
Hiway 120
Cathedral Lks. Tr.

Lower Cathedral Lk. Tr.
Cathedral Pass

Echo Cr. Tr.
Sunrise Camp

181 182 183 184 185 186 187 188 189 190 191 192 193 194 195 196 197 198

10

9

8

7

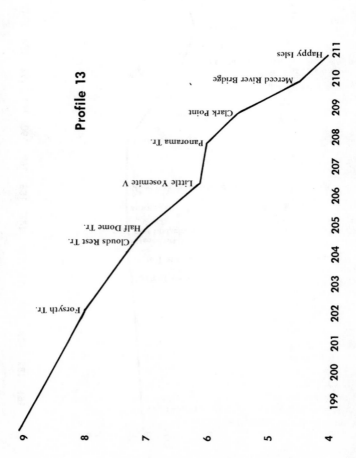

Profile 13

Forsyth Tr.
Clouds Rest Tr.
Half Dome Tr.
Little Yosemite V
Panorama Tr.
Clark Point
Merced River Bridge
Happy Isles

199 200 201 202 203 204 205 206 207 208 209 210 211

Index

Agnew Meadows Trail 54, 76
Arrowhead Lake 25, 83
Aspen Flat 39

Baxter Pass Trail 25, 83
Bear Creek 3, 41, 79
Bear Creek, East Fork 43, 79
Bear Creek, West Fork 41
Bear Ridge 4, 43, 79
bears 5, 6, 57, 65, 73, 76
Bench Lake Trail 26, 82
Big Pete Meadow 32, 80
Bighorn Park 10
Bighorn Plateau 18, 84
Bishop 3
Bishop Pass Trail 30, 80
Blaney Meadows 79
Boundary Creek 48
Bubbs Creek 21, 84
Budd Creek 64
Bullfrog Lake Trail 23, 84

Cartridge Pass Trail 82
Cascade Valley 48, 78
Cascade Valley Trail 45
Cathedral Lake, Lower 65, 74
Cathedral Lake, Upper 65, 74
Cathedral Lakes Trail 65
Cathedral Pass 66, 74
Cedar Grove Trail 23, 84
Center Basin Creek 21
Center Basin Trail 21, 84
Charlotte Lake Trail 23
Chief Lake 45
Clark Point 72
Clouds Rest Trail 70, 74
Colby Meadow 37
Consultation Lake 10, 12
Crabtree Meadows 17, 85
Crabtree Ranger Station 17,
    85

Crater Meadow 48, 78
Crater Meadow, Upper 48, 78

Darwin Canyon 37
Deer Creek 47, 48, 78
Deer Meadow 30, 82
Devils Postpile National
    Monument 50, 77
Dollar Lake 25, 83
Donohue Pass 59, 76
Dragon Lake Trail 25
Duck Creek 47, 78
Duck Lake Trail 47
Dusy Branch 32, 80

Echo Creek 66
Echo Creek Trail 74
Edison, Lake 3, 4
Ediza Lake Trail 54
Emerald Lake 54
Evolution Creek 33, 80
Evolution Lake 33, 80
Evolution Meadow 37, 80
Evolution Valley 37, 80

Fish Creek 45, 78
Florence Lake Trail 39, 41
Forester Pass 21, 84
Forsyth Trail 69, 74

Garnet Lake 54, 76
Glacier Creek 30, 82
Gladys Lake 50, 77
Glen Pass 23, 25, 83, 84
Goddard Divide 33
Goodale Pass Trail 45
Grouse Meadows 30, 80
Guitar Lake 14, 86

Half Dome Trail 70, 73
Happy Isles 1, 71, 72, 73
Heart Lake 41, 79
Helen Lake 33, 80

High Sierra Trail 17
Hilgard Creek 43, 79
Hitchcock Lakes 12

Ireland Creek 76
Island Pass 55

John Muir Wilderness 9
Johnston Meadow 50, 77

Kearsarge Pass Trail 23, 84
King Creek-Clover Meadow
    Trail 50
Kings River, Middle Fork 30,
    80
Kings River, South Fork 21,
    27, 82

Lake Italy Trail 43, 79
Lake South America Trail 18,
    84
Lamarck Col 37
Little Pete Meadow 32, 80
Little Yosemite Valley 71, 73
Lone Pine 9
Lone Pine Creek 10
Lone Pine Lake 10
Long Meadow 66, 74
Lou Beverly Lake 41, 79
Lyell Canyon 59, 76

Mammoth Lakes 4
Mammoth Pass Trail 48
Marie Lake 79
Marie Lakes Trail 57
Marjorie, Lake 26, 82
Mather Pass 27, 82
McClure Meadow 37
McDermand, Lake 33, 80
McGee Pass Trail 45, 78
Merced Lake Trail 70, 71
Merced River 72
Minaret Creek 50, 77
Minaret Lake Trail 50
Mirror Lake 10
Mono Creek 4, 43, 79
Mono Creek, North Fork 43,
    79

Mono Hot Springs 3, 4, 43,
    79
Mono Pass Trail 43, 79
Mt. Whitney Trail 86
Mt. Whitney 1, 2, 9, 12, 14
Muir Pass 33, 80
Muir Trail Ranch 39

Nevada Fall 72, 73
North Lake 3, 39

Onion Valley 23
Outpost Camp 10

Pacific Crest Trail 17, 85
Palisade Creek 30, 80
Palisade Lakes 27, 82
Panorama Trail 72
Pinchot Pass 26, 82
Piute Creek 39
Piute Creek Trail 80
Piute Pass Trail 39
Planning your hike 2
Pocket Meadow 43, 79
Purple Lake 47, 78

Rae Lakes 23, 25, 83
Rafferty Creek 61, 76
Rafferty Creek Trail 61, 76
rangers 6
Red Cones 48, 78
Reds Meadow 4, 48, 49, 77
Rosalie Lake 50, 77
Rose Lake 41, 79
Rosemarie Meadow 41, 79
Ruby Lake 54, 76
Rush Creek Forks 55, 57, 76
Rush Creek Trail 55

Sally Keyes Lakes 41, 79
San Joaquin River, Middle
    Fork 50, 77
Sapphire Lake 33, 34, 80
Sawmill Pass Trail 26, 82
Selden Pass 41, 79
Senger Creek 41, 79
Shadow Creek 52, 77
Shadow Lake 52, 77

Shepherd Pass Trail 18, 84
Silver Pass 45, 78
Silver Pass Creek 45, 78
Silver Pass Lake 45, 78
Simpson Meadow Trail 30, 80
60 Lakes Trail 23, 83
South Fork San Joaquin River
    Trail 38, 80
South Lake 3, 32
Squaw Lake 45, 78
Sunrise Creek 66, 69, 70, 74
Sunrise High Sierra Camp 66,
    74
supplies 2

Taboose Pass Trail 26, 82
1000 Island Lake 54, 76
Timberline Lake 15, 85
Trail Camp 12
Trail Crest 12
Tuolumne Lodge 62, 75
Tuolumne Meadows 1, 3, 4,
    60, 61, 62, 63, 73, 74
Tuolumne River 63, 64, 75
Tuolumne River, Dana Fork
    62

Tuolumne River, Lyell Fork
    60, 62, 76
Trinity Lakes 50, 77
Tully Hole 45, 78
Tyndall Creek 18, 84

Upper Basin 82

Vermilion Valley 43, 79
Vernal Fall 72, 73
Vidette Meadow 21, 23, 84
Virginia, Lake 47, 78

Walker Pass 1
Wallace Creek 17, 85
Wallace Lake 17
Wanda Lake 33, 80
Whitney Creek 17, 85
Whitney Portal 3, 4, 9, 86
Woods Creek 23, 25, 26, 82
Woods Creek, South Fork 25,
    83
Wright Creek 17, 85

Yosemite Valley 1, 3, 4, 9, 72,
    73